CW00322497

WHEEL-IT, RIDE-IT, WOODEN TOYS

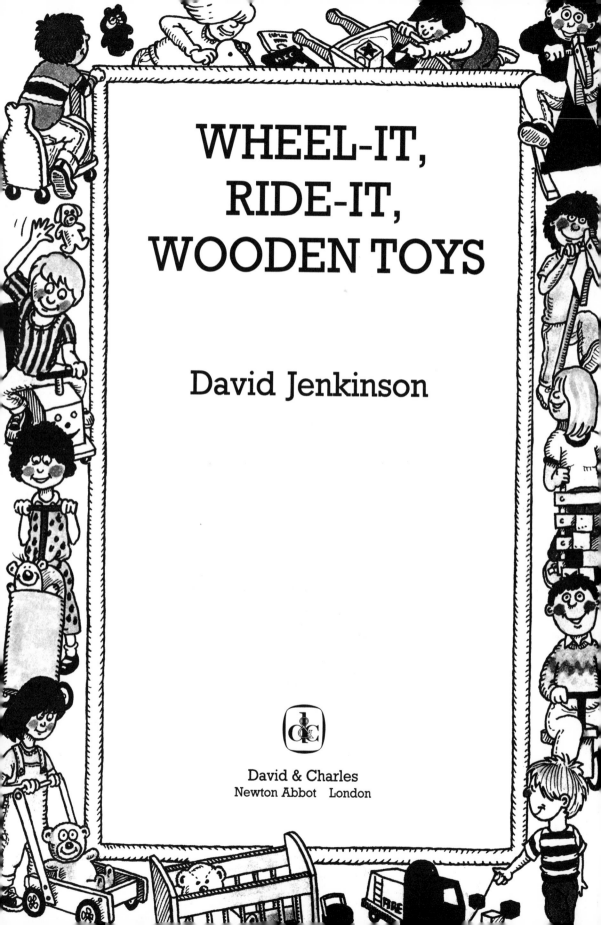

WHEEL-IT, RIDE-IT, WOODEN TOYS

David Jenkinson

David & Charles
Newton Abbot   London

Colour photography by Tony Griffiths, Photography 2000
Jacket design and line drawings by John Headford

British Library Cataloguing in Publication Data
Jenkinson, David
    Wheel-it, ride-it wooden toys.
    1. Wooden toys. Making. Manuals
    I. Title
    745.592

ISBN 0-7153-9197-6

Typeset by Typesetters (Birmingham) Limited
and printed in Great Britain
by Redwood Burn Ltd, Trowbridge, Wiltshire
for David & Charles Publishers plc
Brunel House Newton Abbot Devon

Contents

Acknowledgement

My thanks to West Yorkshire Probation Service and Leeds Community Service Scheme, for their co-operation and encouragement during the writing of this book.

Introduction

This book aims to give the handyman designs for simple-to-make, rideable and push-along wooden toys. Although they are easily constructed, they are very sturdy, and are suitable for both indoor and outdoor play. The toys have all been thoroughly tested for strength, durability, and popularity in playgroups in the Leeds area.

Because of their sturdy construction and the materials used these toys should be safe to use and should have a longer life than many similar commercially produced models, which are often made of plastic. In fact they should be able to be passed on to the next generation, when you consider that these designs have been used to supply toys to playgroups where they get more frequent use than the average household toy.

Another advantage of homemade toys is that they can be personalised for the children by painting their names or initials on them. They can also be further decorated by adding motifs, transfers or stickers.

All the materials used should be readily available at your local timber merchant or DIY store. The toys can be made using basic joinery and DIY hand tools although a few DIY electric power tools would make life a little easier and production a little quicker.

Remember, if these are not readily available they can always be hired.

The handyman can gain a two-fold pleasure from making these toys; firstly you have the self-satisfaction of making a good, sturdy toy; secondly you have the pleasure of watching your child play with the end product.

All the toys included in this book are good for stimulating imaginative and energetic play and should create hours of fun for young children. So have fun making the toys and then relax while your children have fun playing with them.

Handy Hints

Hand Tools

You will need a basic kit of hand tools to carry out the following techniques.

Sawing Tenon saw, coping saw, hacksaw, panel saw.
Marking Ruler, try-square, marking gauge, marking knife, compass.
Shaping Smoothing plane, wood chisels, half-round rasp or file.
Boring Carpenter's brace, auger bits, wheel brace, engineer's bits, bradawl.
Holding and Cramping Sash cramps, G cramps, woodworker's vice and bench, or a workmate.
Miscellaneous Screwdrivers, hammer, nail punch, pincers, cork block.

This is by no means a comprehensive list and only includes the very basics to enable you to make the toys. When building up a collection of tools, very careful consideration should be given to their selection; buying a reputable brand will pay dividends in the long run. A cheap tool may look identical to a more expensive one, but the difference will lie in the quality of materials used in the manufacturing method. The following information was compiled with the help of Stanley Tools and Record Marples Tools.

Tenon saw (back saw)
It is generally used for joint cutting, light bench work and cutting across the grain (sawing to length). The blade is strengthened by a brass or steel back to add rigidity and weight to the saw.

Hand saw
These have a blade length of between 560mm (22in) and 710mm (28in), a rip saw being used to cut with the grain, whilst a cross-cut or panel saw is used for cutting across the gain and cutting sheet material, eg plywood.

Coping saw
A very useful saw for cutting curves in timber of up to 25mm (1in) in thickness. The thin blade is held tight in a sprung frame which can be rotated in the frame.

Wood chisels (1)
Wood chisels are indispensable in the cutting of joints and for shaping wood. They are available in a variety of sizes and styles but the most common in use is the bevel-edged firmer chisel; 6mm (¼in), 12mm (½in) and 18mm (¾in) are the most popular and useful sizes.

Smoothing plane (2)
This is perhaps the most popular and useful

plane for the handyman and is a must to start off your tool kit. A smoothing plane is usually 245mm (9¾in) in length with a blade 50mm (2in) wide which is adjustable for the depth of cut with a lateral adjustment. Many other planes are available, too numerous to mention, for specialist tasks such as rebating, moulding and planing curves.

Honing guide
This is a must for the DIY man for sharpening and honing plane irons and chisels. A blade is set into the guide at the required angle, the guide then enabling the blade to be rolled on an oilstone at the precise angle, thus preventing the rounding off of the bevel.

Rasp
For preliminary rough shaping of both internal and external curves, a half-round one 200mm (8in) long being the most useful.

Surform file
A Surform is a multi-purpose tool which can be used for shaping and smoothing most materials. The blade is so designed to prevent clogging. They are available in various lengths and types and have interchangeable blades – both flat or half-round.

Marking gauge (3)
This is used for marking lines parallel to the edge of a piece of wood.

Mortice gauge
This is similar to the marking gauge but is used to mark two parallel lines to the edge of a piece of wood for marking mortice and tenon joints.

Marking knife
This is particularly useful for marking lines which are to be cut and for marking across the grain of plywoods prior to sawing to help prevent splitting the face veneer.

G cramp (4)
Perhaps the most versatile of all cramping devices, it comes in a variety of sizes and is used for holding work to the bench and for cramping work together while glue sets. To prevent marking the work piece always insert a piece of scrap wood between the work and cramp.

Sash cramps
These are for holding large boards, frames and cabinets together whilst the glue sets. They are available in a variety of sizes, but 915mm (3ft) is an average size. You can make your own using a pair of cramp heads and a length of timber.

Woodworker's vice
These are available in a variety of styles and sizes, and usually need fitting with wooden jaws and mounting on a bench. They are invaluable to all woodworkers allowing for a safer working situation. A vice fitted with a quick release bar is worth the extra expense.

Mallet (5)
Wooden mallets are used for striking chisels when cutting joints rather than using steel hammers.

Bradawl (6)
Its main use is to create small holes for screws and nails.

Hand drill (7)
The hand drill is designed for controlled drilling of small holes and is particularly useful for drilling pilot holes.

Countersink bit (8)
These are used for countersinking holes to receive the head of a screw so that it lies flush with the surface.

Flat bit (9)
These wood-boring bits are designed for use in electric drills and are capable of drilling wood and most other materials at high speed. The hexagonal shank prevents slipping in the drill chuck.

Combination square (10)
A combination square consists of a sliding

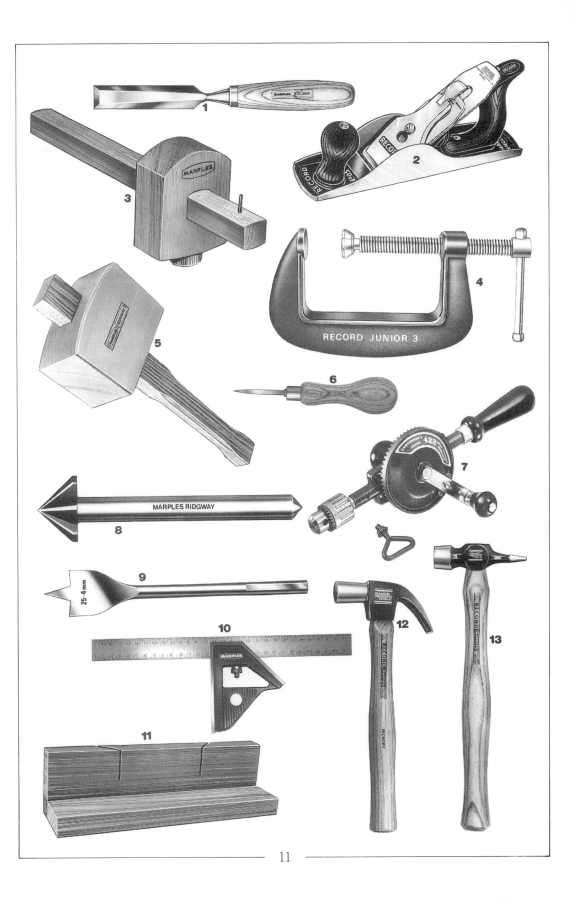

blade in a head and can be used for marking and checking angles of 90° and 45°; it can also be used as a depth gauge and a ruler.

Try square
This consists of a blade riveted to a stock (handle) at an angle of 90° used for marking and checking right angles.

Sliding bevel
This has a blade which is adjustable in the handle through 360° and may be locked into any position. It is used for marking and checking odd angles.

Mitre box or block (11)
These are used for accurate sawing at 45° and 90°.

Hammers
These come in a variety of sizes and styles and are suited to specific tasks.

Claw hammer (12)
This is more suited to rougher joinery work and can also be used for the removal of nails.

Warrington pattern (13)
This is more suited to cabinet-making, carpentry and light benchwork.

Pin hammer
This is a useful addition to any tool kit for those small nails and panel pins.

Do's and don'ts
Don't use any tool for any other purpose than that for which it is intended.

Don't buy cheap, unbranded tools. This is false economy, since they do not usually perform the intended task satisfactorily, and cheap cutting tools, ie saws and chisels, do not retain their sharp cutting edge.

Do make sure that the work in hand is securely cramped to the work bench or held in a vice before starting work on it.

Do store and rack tools in a safe manner

and keep out of reach of children.

Do keep a clean and tidy work bench and work area thus providing a safer working situation.

Don't strike two hammer faces together as these could splinter and cause serious injury.

Don't use broken, damaged, dirty or blunt tools, these could cause damage to your work piece and injury to yourself, as well as requiring more effort to use them.

Do replace guards to cutting edges on tools when not in use.

Power Tools

The wide variety of power tools now available can make many of the tasks much easier, and if the handyman does not own these tools they can usually be hired at a reasonable cost from national DIY stores or local hire firms. An electric drill (use flat bits for large holes) and an electric bench sander will be found most useful. Although not essential an electric jigsaw could prove useful and a router would help in preparing the axle blocks.

A circular, foam-drum sander, which fits into the chuck of all electric drills, is available and is most useful for cleaning up end-grains and internal and external curves on many of the toys to be found in this book.

The following information has been compiled with the help of Black & Decker Power Tools Ltd and is only intended to be a brief guide. Further information should be available from a power tool stockist.

Electric drill (1)
This is perhaps the most common of all power tools and will be found in many homes. A two-speed rotary percussion drill (hammer action) is the most versatile since it can also be used for drilling masonry. Special bits have been developed for use in these drills, ie the flat bit previously mentioned. If you cannot afford some of the other power

tools mentioned you can buy attachments to convert your drill into an orbital sander, jig saw, circular saw or disc sander. The drill can be made more versatile by attaching it to a bench stand. The acquisition of a pillar drill stand will also make it easier and more accurate to drill holes both in position and in depth by using the depth gauge.

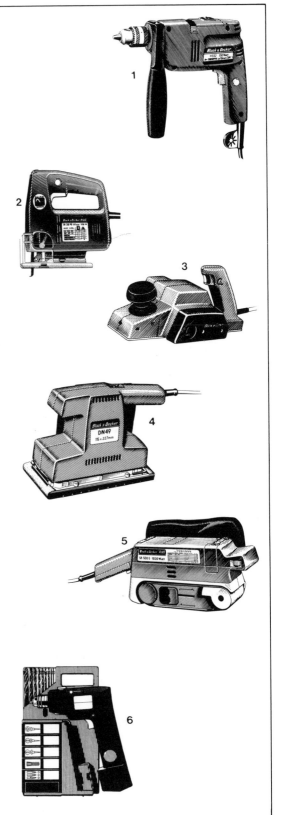

Jig saw (2)
This is a very useful power tool which can be used for cutting straight and curved lines; one with an adjustable sole (base-plate) will also enable you to cut angles.

Electric planer (3)
This can be useful although it can be dangerous in inexperienced hands. It quickly converts rough-sawn timber into planed timber but has limited use. If mounting horizontally on a bench stand ensure that all the correct guards are fitted and are working correctly.

Orbital sander (4)
If involved in a large number of DIY tasks the sander is a must since it will save a great deal of hard work and help to achieve a much better finish. Use different grades of glass paper, starting with a coarse one working down to a fine grit to get the finish required.

Belt sander (5)
A belt sander can sand a rough surface very quickly, but care is needed in its operation. Work sanded with a belt sander will usually require finishing with an orbital sander to get a suitable finish for painting or varnishing. The belt sander is particularly useful if mounted horizontally on a bench enabling the work piece to be offered up to it for rounding corners etc. A sander fitted with a dust extraction bag is much cleaner and comfortable in use.

Cordless drill and screwdriver (6)
These operate with a rechargeable battery and are useful due to their slow speed for screw-driving; they may of course be used for drilling most materials in a situation where a power supply is not available.

Hot melt glue gun

These can be purchased relatively cheaply and use solid glue sticks in a heated gun, the melted glue being squeezed out of a nozzle. They are useful for instant glueing since no cramping is required, but are only suitable for glueing small areas. Be careful as the glue comes out very hot and can give a nasty burn.

Circular saw

A circular saw can be a useful addition to a larger workshop since it will save a great deal of effort in converting timber to size. Many types are available with a variety of accessories and careful thought should be given before buying oner to suit your particular needs.

Band saw

A small bench-mounted band saw would be an invaluable addition to any workshop since their work is so varied for cutting straight lines, curves, angles and some joints.

Power tools are well worth buying or hiring since they can save a great deal of work and help give a more professional finish to your work, but you must realise the potential danger in using any power tool. If you are investing in a new set of power tools it is worth considering purchasing 110v rather than 240v equipment and getting a transformer to convert 240v to 110v. This makes the tools safer to use electrically, and less liable to cause fatal injury should a fault occur, especially in damp conditions. Alternatively to make your existing 240v equipment safe it is worth investing in a power break plug or distribution board in the work shop, which cuts off the power should a fault or damage to the cable occur.

Do's and Don'ts

Don't carry a power tool by its cable.
Don't fit accessories to a power tool for which they are not intended.
Don't let children operate any form of power tool.

Don't wear loose clothing when operating power tools.
Don't adjust any power tool while it is plugged in.

Do read all instructions before using any power tool.
Do make sure the correct size fuse is fitted, and make a regular inspection of all cables and plugs for damage.
Do make sure that the correct guards are fitted to the appropriate machine and that they function properly.
Do make sure that you have a clear, unobstructed work area.
Do use a push stick when using a circular saw.
Do make sure that all power tools are turned off at the mains when not in use.
Do wear the correct protective clothing etc to protect eyes and for protection against excessive dust and noise.

Materials

Plywood

Use a good quality plywood; I have found Malayan red and Russian birch to be the most suitable. When cutting across the grain of plywood it is worth scoring the line to be cut with a marking knife, before sawing slightly on the waste side of the line, to prevent splitting the face veneer. If making the dog, tortoise, or shopping basket, you will find it essential to use birch plywood to enable you to bend it to the shape required.

Timber

Most of the solid timber used on the toys illustrated in the book is Selected European Redwood, which is usually imported from Norway, Finland, Czechoslovakia and Russia. This can be purchased rough sawn or planed. Unless you have access to a planer it is best to purchase your timber ready planed. The timber is usually purchased and known as planed, selected, European redwood, but is commonly known as pine, deal, or just softwood. It will be referred to as planed softwood in the text of this book.

PSE (planed, squared and edged) refers to

timber which is planed on all four sides. If 50 × 25mm (2 × 1in) is bought you will find that it measures approximately 45 × 19mm (1¾ × ¾in). The size refers to the sawn timber size, ie the size before planing. By paying a little extra you may be able to get your timber merchant to cut your timber to size.

Note
Throughout this book, the sizes of timber shown under the list of materials are finished, ie planed sizes.

Screws
The clearance hole is the size of hole to be drilled for the shank of the screw. The pilot hole is the drill size for the thread of the screw (this is only normally drilled when screwing into hardwoods, difficult timbers, or occasionally into end-grains). It is sometimes advisable to lubricate the screw threads to facilitate easy entry into hardwoods. This is best done by dipping the screw tip into vaseline or furniture wax. Use the table given below to drill the correct hole size for the gauge of screw you are using.

Surface screwcups are useful since they enhance the appearance, and save the trouble of counter sinking and having to fill the screw hole with woodfiller.

Screw Hole Sizes

Gauge of screw	Clearance hole		Pilot hole	
	Inch	mm	Inch	mm
4	1/8	3	5/64	2
6	5/32	4	5/64	2
8	3/16	5	3/32	2.5
10	7/32	5.5	1/8	3
12	1/4	6	1/8	3

Wood filler
Throughout the making of the toys it will be found necessary to fill pin holes, joints and discrepancies in the timber. Where these are to be filled in wood which is to be varnished they should be filled with a natural-coloured woodfiller, or one which suits the colour of the wood.

However, where holes and cracks are to be filled on areas which are to be painted it is easier and quicker to use one of the modern paste-type fillers which are mixed with a catalyst hardener (the type of filler usually associated with car body repairs). This filler is particularly useful since it sets quickly without shrinking and is easily sanded to a smooth finish.

Finishing
Remember that the finishing of an item can 'make or break' a job and is the difference between a good or bad toy. Take your time in finishing your toy, taking care in the preparation and sanding before painting.

Glass-papering
Before painting or varnishing it is necessary to sand all the surfaces to a smooth finish, after filling any imperfections. When preparing wood for a varnished finish glass-papering must be carried out in the direction of the grain to avoid scratching; use a cork block or an electric sander where possible. Start by using a medium grit glass-paper followed by a finer one. Garnet paper will be found more effective and economical, although it is a little more expensive than glass-paper. Where a toy is in several pieces, eg the train, it will be found much easier to paint or varnish the pieces separately before final assembly.

Painting
Ensure that all the areas to be painted are all filled, where necessary, and sanded. Try to select a dust-free atmosphere for painting and ensure that you use a lead-free, non-toxic paint. Most modern well-known paints are safe to use on children's toys and furniture, but if in any doubt check with your stockist. Some manufacturers have recently developed paints solely for this purpose and it may be worth paying a little extra for this.

Follow the instructions given with the paint, but in general two undercoats and two coats of gloss will be required. It will be necessary to lightly rub down the work between coats and to dust down before re-coating.

Varnishing

Use a suitable clear varnish to protect and enhance the timber which is to be left natural. You may also varnish over painted surfaces, transfers and stickers.

After careful sanding, dust down and apply one coat of varnish. A light rub down, with the grain, is necessary between each coat of varnish. Follow the instructions on the tin, but you will find that three or four coats are necessary.

Wheels

The method of fitting the wheels is common to most of the toys in this book and detailed instructions are given in the appropriate chapters. Check the dimensions of the wheels before cutting the parts needed for wheel fitting, since these will depend upon the size of wheel available, and therefore the size of axle to be used. This will also determine the size of the groove to be machined in the axle blocks, or the diameter of the hole to be drilled to accept the axle.

100mm (4in) diameter wheels with a 10mm ($\frac{3}{8}$in) diameter steel axle were used on the wheeled toys illustrated in this book.

In all cases the wheels are held on the axles by using push-on, sprung, hub-caps; these should be readily available at most DIY outlets, but may be known by different names. Care must be taken when screwing the axle blocks to the toys to avoid splitting the block, or obstructing the groove in the block.

Castors

I have found a good quality 45mm ($1\frac{3}{4}$in) twin-wheeled, plate-fitting castor to be most satisfactory on all the toys fitted with castors, but have a good look round to see what is available. A rubber-tyred castor is available and is perhaps more suited to rougher outdoor use.

Castors are now usually sold pre-packed in sets of four and include the fixing screws and instructions. If you can buy them loose they may be cheaper.

Train

The train is always a popular toy with children. Everyone will want to be the engine driver! Like several of the toys in this book it is made up from three easy-to-make sections, the tank, the cab and the base. The addition of castors makes the train easily manoeuvrable without the difficulty of fitting a steering system to the front. It is exceptionally durable and when painted in bright colours with the addition of a face on the front, will give your child hours of fun and pleasure.
(Shown in colour on page 33)

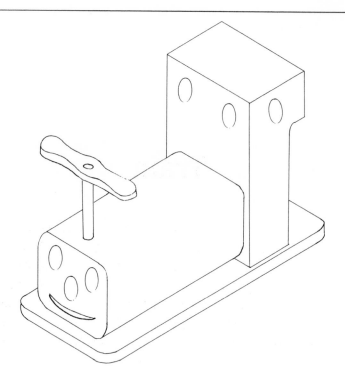

Fig 1 Assembled train

Materials

Tank (Fig 3)
Sides	2	380 × 146 × 19mm (15 × 5³/₄ × ³/₄in)	Planed softwood
Top	1	380 × 197 × 19mm (15 × 7³/₄ × ³/₄in)	Planed softwood
Bottom	1	380 × 197 × 19mm (15 × 7³/₄ × ³/₄in)	Planed softwood
Front	1	203 × 203 × 6mm (8 × 8 × ¹/₄in)	Plywood
Hand support	1	355 × 25mm (14 × 1in)	Dowel
Handle	1	255 × 50 × 25mm (10 × 2 × 1in)	Plywood

Cab (Fig 8)
Sides	2	355 × 152 × 12mm (14 × 6 × ¹/₂in)	Plywood
Front	1	355 × 216 × 12mm (14 × 8¹/₂ × ¹/₂in)	Plywood
Top	1	216 × 165 × 12mm (8¹/₂ × 6¹/₂ × ¹/₂in)	Plywood

Base (Fig 9)
Base	1	610 × 255 × 19mm (24 × 10 × ³/₄in)	Plywood

4 × 45mm (1³/₄in) twin-wheeled, plate-fitting castors
40mm (1¹/₂in) no 8 countersunk woodscrews
19mm (³/₄in) no 6 roundheaded woodscrews
No 8 surface screwcups
25mm (1in) and 32mm (1¹/₄in) panel pins
Wood glue
Woodfiller
Non-toxic undercoat and gloss paints
Clear varnish

Tank

1 Glue and cramp the four pieces of planed softwood together to form a box (Fig 2) and leave overnight to set. If cramps are not available it is possible to glue and nail the tank together, using 50mm (2in) oval nails, which should later be punched in and filled with a suitable natural woodfiller. If the tank has been nailed together, care must be taken when rounding off the corners.

2 When the glue has set, the tank may be cleaned up and the corners rounded off using a smoothing plane, cork block and glass-paper. Glue and pin the plywood front in place, punch in the pins and fill the holes. Drill a 25mm (1in) diameter hole, for the dowel handle support, in the top and bottom of the tank in the position indicated (Fig 3).

3 Make the handle from a piece of 25mm (1in) plywood. If this is not available it is possible

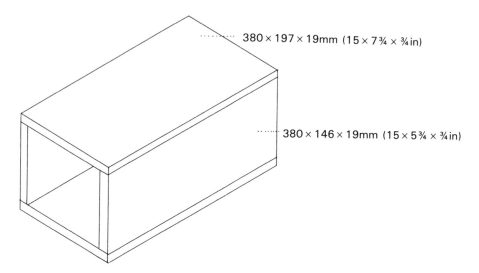

380 × 197 × 19mm (15 × 7¾ × ¾ in)

380 × 146 × 19mm (15 × 5¾ × ¾ in)

Fig 2 Tank unit glued together

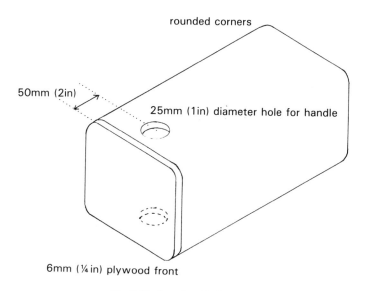

rounded corners

50mm (2in)

25mm (1in) diameter hole for handle

6mm (¼ in) plywood front

Fig 3 Tank unit with front in place

19

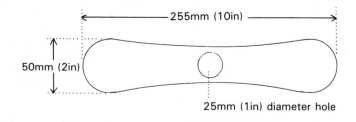

255mm (10in)

50mm (2in)

25mm (1in) diameter hole

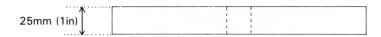

25mm (1in)

Fig 4 Handle top and side view

Fig 5 Dowel handle showing position of wedges

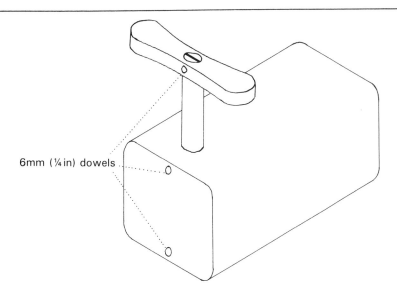

6mm (¼ in) dowels

Fig 6 Tank with handle in position

to glue together two pieces of 12mm (½in) plywood to achieve the required thickness. Drill a 25mm (1in) diameter hole through the centre of the wood, and cut to shape, using an electric jigsaw or coping saw. Shape the handle to form a comfortable grip, rounding off all the corners using a rasp or file and glass paper (Fig 4).

4 Use a tenon saw to put a saw cut in each end of the 25mm (1in) dowel (Fig 5) to a depth of about 19mm (³/₄in).

5 Put the dowel through the holes already made in the tank and glue a wedge into the bottom saw cut. The handle is fastened to the dowel in the same way. For extra security drill a 6mm (¹/₄in) diameter hole through the tank front and dowel handle, and glue a short length of dowel into the holes (Fig 6).

6 Clean up the whole tank unit with glass-paper in readiness for fitting to the cab and base at a later stage.

Cab

7 Cut out the cab sides, top and front from four pieces of 12mm (¹/₂in) plywood (Fig 7).

8 Drill two 25mm (1in) diameter holes in each side section and two in the front (Fig 7) and then use an electric jigsaw or tenon saw to cut the sides to shape and clean up with glass-paper, removing all sharp edges.

9 Pin and glue the front to the sides, and then pin and glue the top in place (Fig 8). All the pins should be punched in and filled.

10 Drill four 5mm (³/₁₆in) holes in the front of the cab, in a suitable position to enable it to be screwed to the tank at a later stage. Clean up with glass-paper.

Base

11 Prepare a piece of 19mm (³/₄in) plywood, to the size shown (Fig 9) by rounding off the four corners and sanding all the edges

12 Drill four 5mm (³/₁₆in) diameter holes, clearance for no 8 woodscrews, in a suitable position to enable the tank to be screwed to the base. Countersink these holes.

13 Using 19mm (³/₄in) no 6 roundheaded woodscrews (these may be supplied with the castors), screw the castor plates onto each corner of the base.

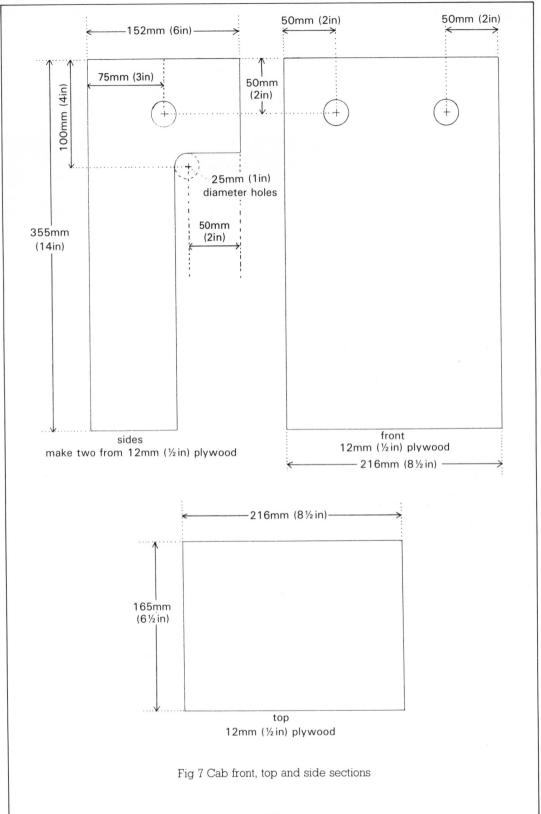

Fig 7 Cab front, top and side sections

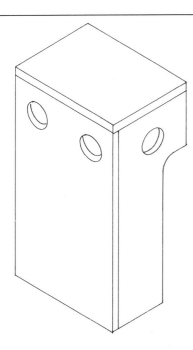

Finishing

14 Before painting screw all the parts together, and then dismantle them, as this makes it easier to assemble the parts once they have been painted.

15 After a final clean up with glass-paper, paint and varnish the appropriate parts, painting a face on the front of the tank. Use non-toxic paints and varnish.

16 Fasten the tank to the base using 40mm ($1\frac{1}{2}$in) no 8 countersunk woodscrews.

17 Screw the cab to the tank using 40mm ($1\frac{1}{2}$in) no 8 countersunk woodscrews with screw cups.

18 Finally fit the castors to the plates.

Fig 8 Assembled cab

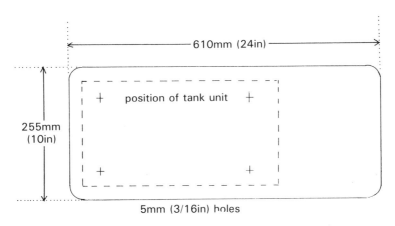

610mm (24in)

255mm (10in)

position of tank unit

5mm (3/16in) holes

Fig 9 Base cut from 18mm ($^3/_4$in) plywood

Rocking Crib

This is an attractive crib for your child's favourite doll. Once equipped with blankets and a pillow, the doll or teddy can be tucked in and rocked to sleep. The crib is easy to make, in sections, and the dimensions can be altered, in proportion, to suit the size of your child's dolls. I have varnished the crib but you may like to paint it in white or pastel colours.
(Shown in colour on page 34)

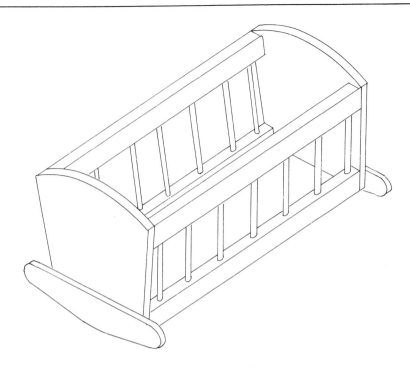

Fig 1 Assembled crib

Materials

Ends	2	255 × 255 × 12mm (10 × 10 × $^1/_2$in)	Plywood
Rockers	2	305 × 75 × 12mm (12 × 3 × $^1/_2$in)	Plywood
Rails	4	510 × 40 × 19mm (20 × $1^1/_2$ × $^3/_4$in)	Planed softwood
Base	1	533 × 203 × 6mm (21 × 8 × $^1/_4$in)	Plywood
Bars	14	178 × 9mm (7 × $^3/_8$in)	Birch dowel

50mm (2in) no 8 countersunk woodscrews
No 8 surface screwcups
19mm ($^3/_4$in) panel pins
Wood glue
Clear varnish

1 Cut out the two ends and two rockers from the pieces of 12mm ($^1/_2$in) plywood to the size and shape shown (Fig 2).
2 Drill the holes as shown, 5mm ($^3/_{16}$in) diameter, clearance for no 8 woodscrews. Ensure that the holes in the rockers correspond to the position of the lower holes in the crib ends.
3 Clean these four pieces up and remove all sharp edges.

4 Cramp the four pieces (rails) of 40 × 19mm ($1^1/_2$ × $^3/_4$in) softwood together in the vice and square the lines across each piece to mark the centre of the holes (Fig 3).
5 Separate the pieces and, using a marking gauge, 'gauge' a centre line (Fig 3) across the thickness of the wood.
6 Drill seven 9mm ($^3/_8$in) diameter holes to a depth of 19mm ($^3/_4$in) in each rail. It is advisable to set up some type of depth gauge

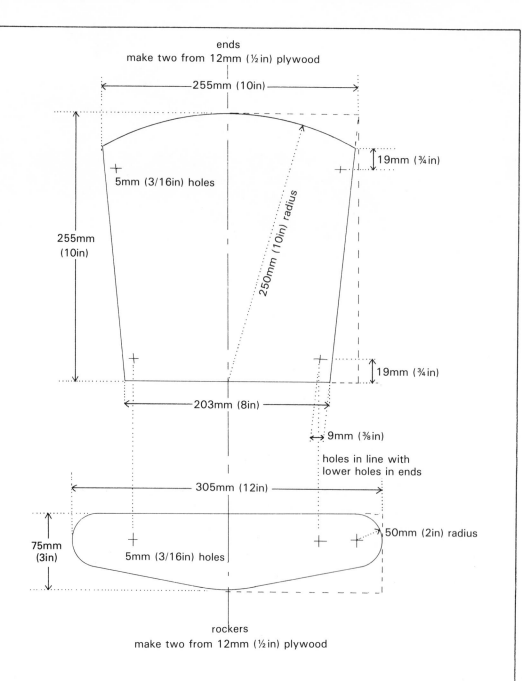

ends
make two from 12mm (½in) plywood

255mm (10in)

19mm (¾in)

5mm (3/16in) holes

250mm (10in) radius

255mm (10in)

19mm (¾in)

203mm (8in)

9mm (⅜in)

holes in line with
lower holes in ends

305mm (12in)

50mm (2in) radius

75mm (3in)

5mm (3/16in) holes

rockers
make two from 12mm (½in) plywood

Fig 2 Cutting plan for ends and rockers

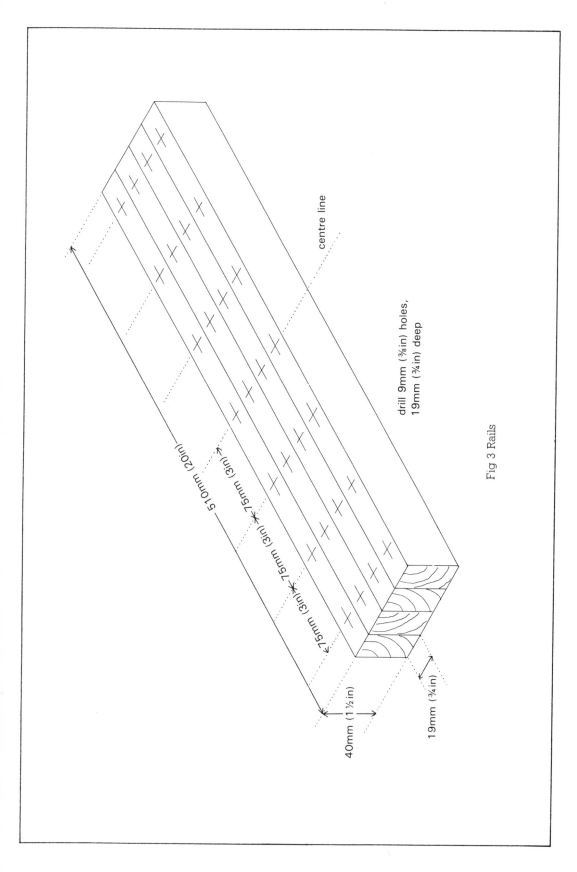

510mm (20in)

75mm (3in) 75mm (3in) 75mm (3in) 75mm (3in)

40mm (1½in)

19mm (¾in)

centre line

drill 9mm (⅜in) holes,
19mm (¾in) deep

Fig 3 Rails

on your drill for this purpose.

7 Remove all the sharp edges from the side rails, and clean up the rails using glass-paper before assembly.

8 Assemble the side frames by inserting the dowels into the holes to make up the two sides. Check on the length of the dowels; the side frames should match the slope length of the crib ends. It is not necessary to glue these dowels in place since the frames cannot move once screwed to the ends.

9 Using 50mm (2in) no 8 countersunk wood-screws and screwcups, glue and screw the ends and rockers to the side frames.

10 Cut out the base from a piece of 6mm ($^1/_4$in) plywood.

11 Clean up with glass-paper.

12 Glue and pin the base to the bottom of the crib using 19mm ($^3/_4$in) panel pins.

Finishing

13 Thoroughly clean up the entire crib using glass-paper.

14 Apply three or four coats of clear varnish.

Pram/Baby Carriage

How could your child's favourite doll or teddy be taken for a walk without this to ride in? Children love copying adults and what better way to encourage walking in the park or garden than with the aid of this toy. The addition of a few homemade sheets and covers will make it much more appealing and create hours of play activity for the small child.

(Shown in colour on page 34)

Fig 1 Assembled pram/baby carriage

Materials

Ends	2	305 × 216 × 19mm (12 × 8½ × ¾in)	Planed softwood
Sides	2	455 × 150 × 12mm(18 × 6 × ½in)	Plywood
Bottom	1	255 × 406 × 6mm(10 × 16 × ¼in)	Plywood
Handle supports		508 × 45 × 19mm (20 × 1¾ × ¾in)	Planed softwood
Handle	1	25mm(1in)	Dowel
Axle blocks	2	305 × 45 × 45mm (12 × 1¾ × 1¾in)	Planed softwood
Wheels	4	100mm(4in) diameter	
Axles	2	made from 355mm(14in) steel bar to suit wheels	

45mm(1¾in) no 8 countersunk woodscrews
32mm(1¼in) no 8 countersunk woodscrews
25mm(1in) no 8 countersunk woodscrews
No 8 surface screwcups
25mm(1in) panel pins
6mm(¼in) dowel
Wood glue
Clear varnish
Sprung hub-caps

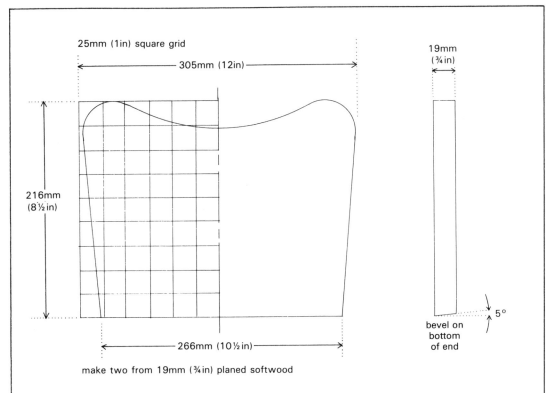

25mm (1in) square grid

305mm (12in)

19mm (¾in)

216mm (8½in)

266mm (10½in)

5°

bevel on bottom of end

make two from 19mm (¾in) planed softwood

Fig 2 Cutting plan for ends

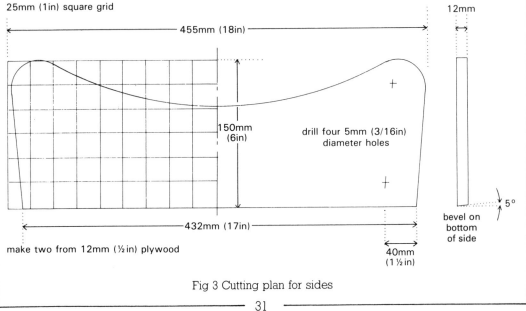

25mm (1in) square grid

455mm (18in)

12mm

150mm (6in)

drill four 5mm (3/16in) diameter holes

432mm (17in)

5°

bevel on bottom of side

make two from 12mm (½in) plywood

40mm (1½in)

Fig 3 Cutting plan for sides

1 Cut out the ends of the pram body from the 216 × 19mm (8½ × ¾in) planed softwood.
2 Use a coping saw or electric jigsaw to cut and shape the curves, and a tenon saw or electric jigsaw to cut the angled ends (Fig 2).
3 Plane the ends and clean up the curves using a wood rasp or file and glass-paper.
4 Cut the shape of the two sides, using two pieces of 12mm (½in) plywood (Fig 3).
5 Drill four (5mm (³/₁₆in) diameter holes in each piece as indicated (clearance hole for no 8 woodscrews).
6 Plane a bevel on the bottom edge of all the body pieces to allow for the sides and ends being angled, this angle being 85°.
7 Clean up and sand all the body pieces and then glue and screw them together using 45mm (1¾in) no 8 countersunk woodscrews and no 8 surface screwcups.
8 Cut out the pram bottom from 6mm (¼in) plywood.
9 Pin and glue the bottom in place using 25mm (1in) panel pins, trim off any over-hanging edges using a smoothing plane and remove all sharp edges with glass-paper.

10 Make the axle blocks from two pieces of 45 × 45mm (1¾ × 1¾in) planed softwood. Leave it in one length until the groove has been machined down its length to accept the steel axle (Fig 4).

This may be done in several ways, either by using an electric router, a plough plane, or by taking several cuts out on a circular saw, providing you have access to one with a rise and fall table. If none of these methods is available, it is possible to make two saw cuts with a tenon saw, and then remove the waste using a wood chisel of the correct width.
11 Position the axle blocks accurately on the bottom, and screw on with care using 25mm (1in) no 8 countersunk woodscrews and screwcups. Avoid splitting the sides of the block and damaging the groove.
12 Prepare the two pieces of 45 × 19mm (1¾ × ¾in) planed softwood for the handle supports (Fig 5). Shape the bottom end of each one to fit the bottom of the pram, as the sides are already at a slope of 5°. Round off the top of each piece and drill a 25mm (1in) diameter hole to accept the dowel handle.

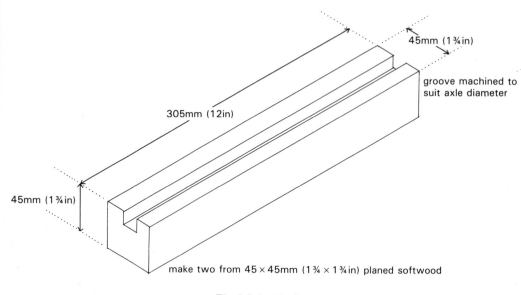

45mm (1¾in)

groove machined to suit axle diameter

305mm (12in)

45mm (1¾in)

make two from 45 × 45mm (1¾ × 1¾in) planed softwood

Fig 4 Axle blocks

colour photograph:
Train (page 17)

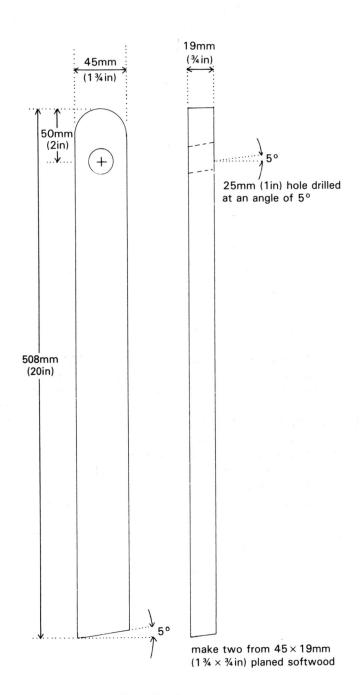

45mm
(1 ¾ in)

19mm
(¾ in)

50mm
(2in)

508mm
(20in)

5°

25mm (1in) hole drilled
at an angle of 5°

5°

make two from 45 × 19mm
(1 ¾ × ¾ in) planed softwood

Fig 5 Handle supports

colour photograph:
Pram/Baby Carriage (page 29) and Rocking Crib
(page 24)

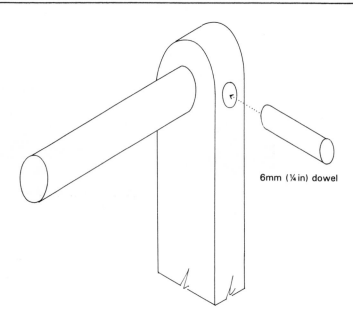

6mm (¼ in) dowel

Fig 6 Secure dowel handle to support

Note Since the handle supports slope outwards the holes must not be drilled at right angles to the supports but at an angle of 85° (Fig 5).

13 Clean up and sand the handle supports.

14 Drill the sides of the pram to correspond to the handle positions, using a 5mm ($^3/_{16}$in) drill, to take 32mm ($1^1/_4$in) × no 8 countersunk woodscrews and screwcups and glue and screw the handle supports to the inside of the pram.

15 Make the handle from a piece of 25mm (1in) dowel and secure it in position by drilling a 6mm ($^1/_4$in) diameter hole through the support into the dowel. Peg it with a piece of 6mm (¼in) dowel (Fig 6) and glue it in place.

Finishing

16 Clean up the whole of the pram with glass-paper.

17 Apply three or four coats of varnish.

18 Fit the wheels, and use sprung hub-caps to hold the wheels on the axles.

Baby Walker

This traditional design is exceptionally sturdy and will last the small child for many years. It is not only an aid to walking, but is useful for the storage and transportation of other toys. I have used clear varnish to show off the natural wood but you can, of course, paint it in bright colours. Why not add your child's name and make this toy a special present.
(Shown in colour on page 53)

Fig 1 Assembled baby walker

Materials

Ends	2	280 × 146 × 19mm(11 × 5¾ × ¾in)	Planed softwood
Sides	2	508 × 100 × 19mm(20 × 4 × ¾in)	Planed softwood
Bottom	1	406 × 317 × 6mm(16 × 12½ × ¼in)	Plywood
Handle supports	2	508 × 45 × 19mm(20 × 1¾ × ¾in)	Planed softwood
Handle	1	356 × 25mm(14 × 1in)	Dowel
Axle blocks	2	330 × 45 × 45mm(13 × 1¾ × 1¾in)	Planed softwood

4 × 100mm(1in) diameter plastic wheels
Steel axle to suit wheels
Sprung hub-caps
50mm(2in) no 8 countersunk woodscrews
40mm(1½in) no 8 countersunk woodscrews
25mm(1in) no 8 countersunk woodscrews
No 8 surface screwcups
25mm (1in) panel pins
Wood glue
6mm(¼in) dowel
Clear varnish

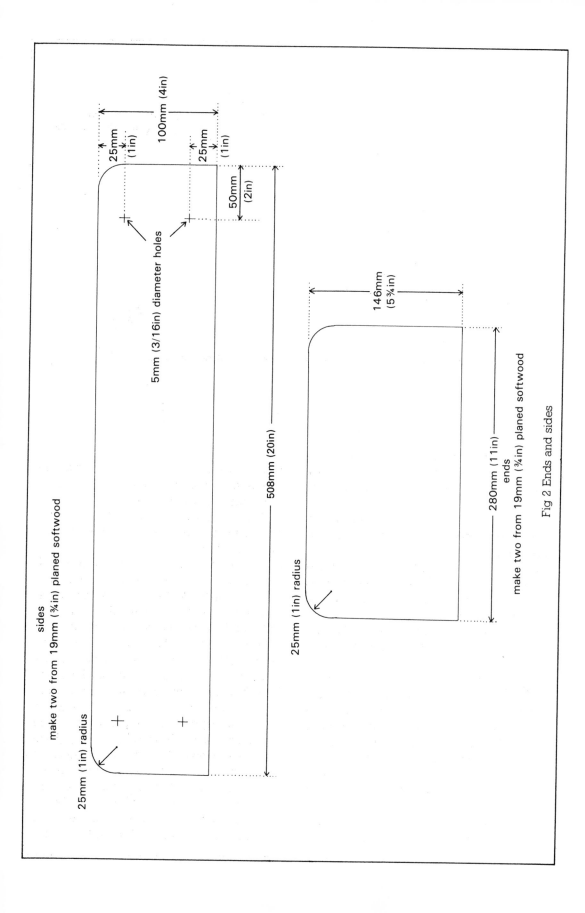

sides
make two from 19mm (¾in) planed softwood

25mm (1in) radius

5mm (3/16in) diameter holes

25mm (1in)

100mm (4in)

25mm (1in)

50mm (2in)

508mm (20in)

146mm (5¾in)

25mm (1in) radius

280mm (11in)
ends
make two from 19mm (¾in) planed softwood

Fig 2 Ends and sides

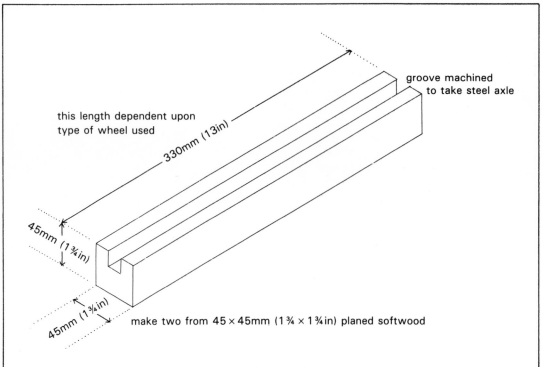

this length dependent upon
type of wheel used

330mm (13in)

45mm (1 ¾ in)

45mm (1 ¾ in)

groove machined
to take steel axle

make two from 45 × 45mm (1 ¾ × 1 ¾ in) planed softwood

Fig 3 Axle blocks

1 Prepare the two ends and the two sides from the 19mm ($^3/_4$in) planed softwood, by rounding off the two top corners of each piece (Fig 2).

2 Drill four 5mm ($^3/_{16}$in) diameter holes, clearance for no 8 woodscrews, in each side piece (Fig 2).

3 Clean up all the inner and outer faces of the ends and sides before assembly as these are inaccessible once the unit has been assembled.

4 Glue and screw the sides to the ends using 50mm (2in) no 8 countersunk woodscrews and screwcups.

5 Glue the 6mm ($^1/_4$in) plywood bottom in place and pin with 25mm (1in) panel pins.

6 Make the two axle blocks from two pieces of 45 × 45mm ($1^3/_4$ × $1^3/_4$in) planed softwood (Fig 3). Plough a groove, the width of the axle to be used, down the length of each piece. This may be done in several ways, either by using an electric router, a plough plane, or by taking several cuts out with a circular saw, providing you have access to one with a rise and fall table. If none of these methods

is available, it is possible to make two saw cuts with a tenon saw, and then remove the waste using a wood chisel.

7 Drill the plywood bottom to take no 8 countersunk woodscrews, in the positions indicated (Fig 4).

8 Use 25mm (1in) no 8 countersunk woodscrews and no 8 screwcups to glue and screw the axle blocks to the plywood base, taking care not to split the sides and not to obstruct the groove in the axle blocks.

9 Prepare the handle supports, using two pieces of 45 × 19mm ($1^3/_4$ × $^3/_4$in) planed softwood. Shape the ends and drill a 25mm (1in) hole through the top of each piece (Fig 5).

10 Drill two 5mm ($^3/_{16}$in) holes in the lower ends of the supports and use 40mm ($1^1/_2$in) no 8 countersunk woodscrews and screwcups to screw the handle supports to the outside of the body. Care must be taken when fastening the handle supports to the body to ensure that they do not foul the wheels. It is better to temporarily put a wheel in place while screwing the supports to the body. Precise

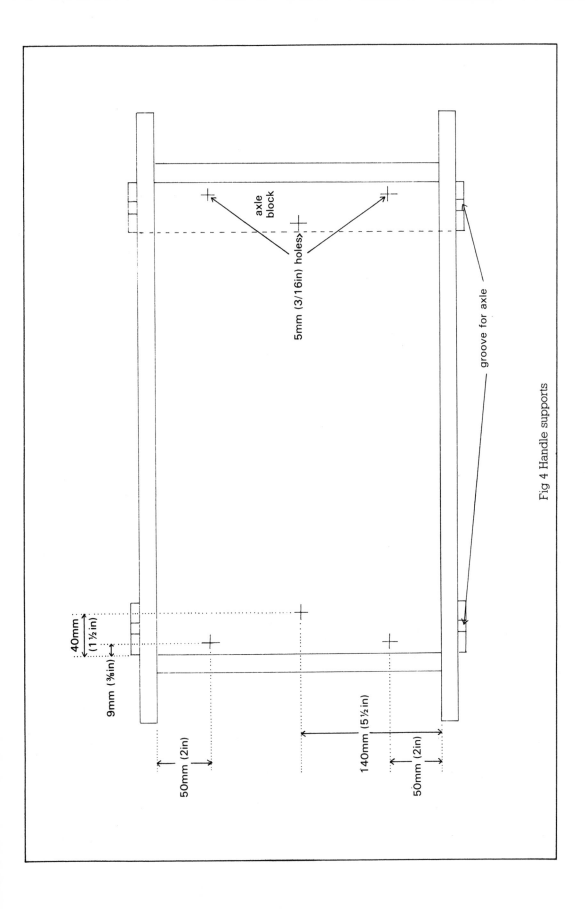

Fig 4 Handle supports

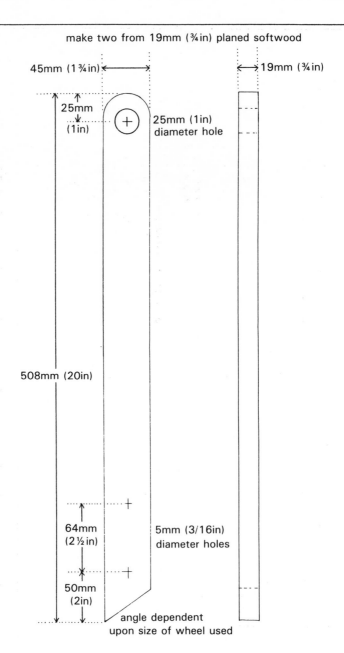

make two from 19mm (¾in) planed softwood

45mm (1¾in)

19mm (¾in)

25mm (1in)

25mm (1in) diameter hole

508mm (20in)

64mm (2½in)

5mm (3/16in) diameter holes

50mm (2in)

angle dependent upon size of wheel used

Fig 5 Dowel handle and support

measurements and positions of these supports are not given since these will ultimately depend on the wheel size, and the height of the child to use the toy.

11 Secure the 25mm (1in) dowel handle in place by drilling a 6mm (¼in) diameter hole through the support into the dowel, and then glue and peg with 6mm (¼in) dowel (Fig 6).

Finishing

12 Clean up thoroughly with glass-paper.

13 Apply three or four coats of clear varnish.

14 Finally, fit the wheels using sprung hubcaps to hold the wheels on the axles.

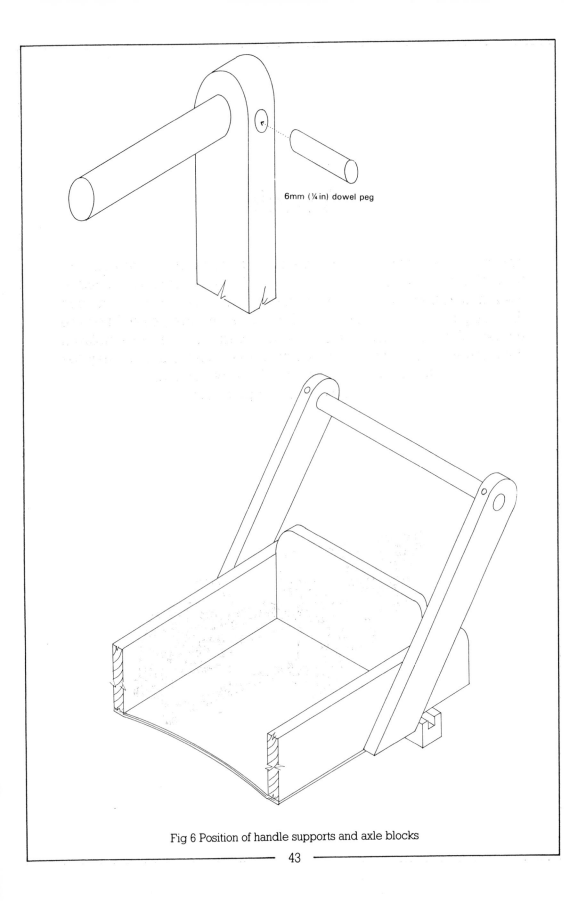

6mm (¼ in) dowel peg

Fig 6 Position of handle supports and axle blocks

43

Truck

This is a particularly sturdy toy made up from easily assembled sections. The back of the truck has hinged doors allowing your child to load up and then deliver toys around the play area. You can modify the design to that of an open truck if you wish. The possibilities are endless! Paint the truck in your child's favourite colours, or emblazon their name on the side, then sit back and see how much fun they get from running their own delivery service!

(Shown in colour on page 51)

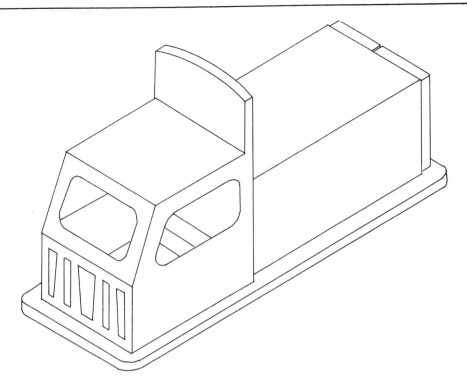

Fig 1 Assembled truck

Materials

Back unit (Fig 2)
Sides	2	380 × 146 × 19mm(15 × 5¾ × ¾in)	Planed softwood
Top	1	380 × 197 × 19mm(15 × 7¾ × ¾in)	Planed softwood
Doors	2	153 × 95 × 19mm(6 × 3¾ × ¾in)	Planed softwood
Bottom blocks	2	159 × 45 × 45mm(6¼ × 1¾ × 1¾in)	Planed softwood

Cab (Fig 6)
Sides	2	255 × 255 × 12mm(10 × 10 × ½in)	Plywood
Back	1	380 × 216 × 12mm(15 × 8½ × ½in)	Plywood
Top	1	216 × 203 × 12mm(8½ × 8 × ½in)	Plywood
Front	1	216 × 127 × 12mm(8½ × 5 × ½in)	Plywood
Windscreen	1	216 × 152 × 12mm(8½ × 6 × ½in)	Plywood
Bottom blocks	2	190 × 45 × 45(7½ × 1¾ × 1¾in)	Planed softwood

Base (Fig 8)
Base	1	710 × 255 × 19mm(28 × 10 × ¾in)	Plywood

4 × 45mm(1¾in) twin-wheeled, plate-fitting castors
Piano hinge approximately 305mm (12in)
Small gate hook
40mm(1½in) no 8 countersunk woodscrews

40mm(1¹/₂in) no 6 countersunk woodscrews
12mm(¹/₂in) no 4 countersunk woodscrews (for piano hinges)
19mm(³/₄in) no 6 roundheaded woodscrews (for castor plates)
No 6 surface screwcups
40mm(1¹/₂in) oval nails
32mm(1¹/₄in) panel pins
Wood glue
Woodfiller
Non-toxic undercoat and gloss paints
Clear varnish

Back

1 Cut out the sides and top, glue and nail the three pieces of planed softwood together using 40mm (1¹/₂in) oval nails (Fig 2).
2 Cut two pieces of 45 × 45mm (1³/₄ × 1³/₄in) timber as bottom blocks (Fig 2).
3 Glue and nail the top to the sides, and then glue and nail the blocks in place.
4 Punch in all the nails and fill the holes with a natural woodfiller. Clean up and glass-paper the whole back unit ensuring that all the sharp edges are removed and slightly rounded off.
5 Using two pieces of piano hinge, hinge two pieces of suitably sized, 19mm (³/₄in) thick, planed timber on the back of the unit to form the doors (Fig 3). These may be held closed by using a small gate hook.

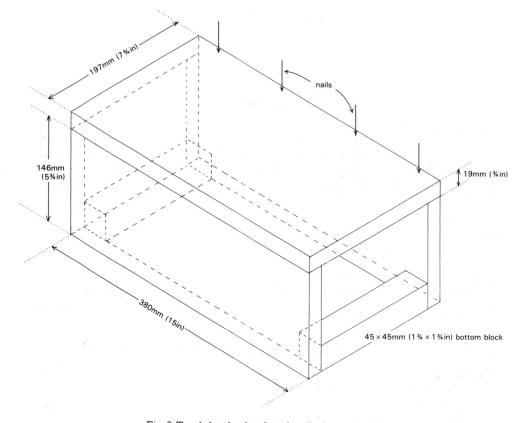

197mm (7³/₄in)

nails

146mm (5³/₄in)

19mm (³/₄in)

380mm (15in)

45 × 45mm (1³/₄ × 1³/₄in) bottom block

Fig 2 Truck back glued and nailed together

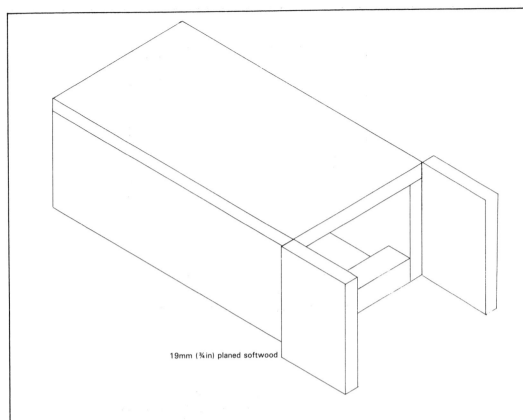

19mm (¾in) planed softwood

Fig 3 Back doors hinged in place

Cab

6 The cab is constructed from six pieces of 12mm ($\frac{1}{2}$in) plywood, and two pieces of 45 × 45mm ($1\frac{3}{4} \times 1\frac{3}{4}$in) planed softwood. Cut the back, top, two sides, front and windscreen from the plywood, to the sizes shown (Fig 4).
7 Cut the windows in the side panels by drilling four 25mm (1in) diameter holes, using a flat bit in an electric drill, in the positions indicated (Fig 5). Cut between the holes using an electric jigsaw or coping saw, but maintain the curve in the corners. It is advisable here to score the lines to be cut across the grain of the plywood with a marking knife, and to saw just on the waste side of the lines. This is to help prevent splitting the face veneer of the plywood when cutting across the grain.
8 Clean up the sawn edges of the window apertures using glass-paper, and if necessary a rasp or file.
9 Glue and pin together the cab using 32mm (1$\frac{1}{4}$in) panel pins which should be punched in and filled. Begin by pinning the back to the sides, followed by the top A and then the front B. The front edge of the top should be bevelled off to suit the slope of the front where the windscreen is to fit (Fig 6).
10 The size of the windscreen is finally determined by the length of the slope previously cut on the sides of the cab, and must be fitted accordingly, the bottom edge of which must be bevelled to fit the top edge of the lower front, indicated at C (Fig 6).
11 Cut out the windows repeating the technique used for making the windows in the side panels (Fig 7).
12 Glue and pin the two bottom blocks (D and E) of 45 × 45mm ($1\frac{3}{4} \times 1\frac{3}{4}$in) planed softwood to the inside of the cab (Fig 6). This is to enable the cab to be secured to the base at a later stage.
13 Drill two 4mm ($\frac{5}{32}$in) diameter holes

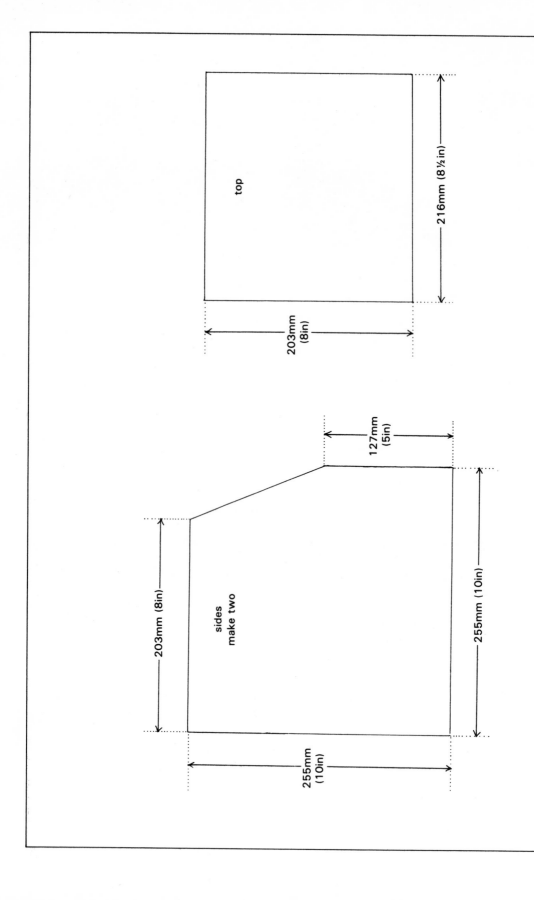

top

203mm
(8in)

216mm (8½ in)

127mm
(5in)

203mm (8in)

sides
make two

255mm (10in)

255mm
(10in)

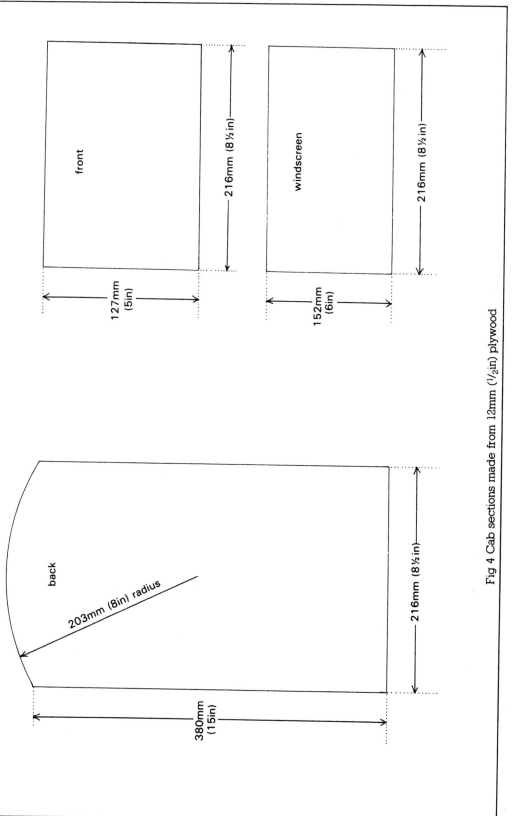

front

216mm (8½ in)

127mm (5in)

windscreen

216mm (8½ in)

152mm (6in)

back

203mm (8in) radius

216mm (8½ in)

380mm (15in)

Fig 4 Cab sections made from 12mm ($\frac{1}{2}$in) plywood

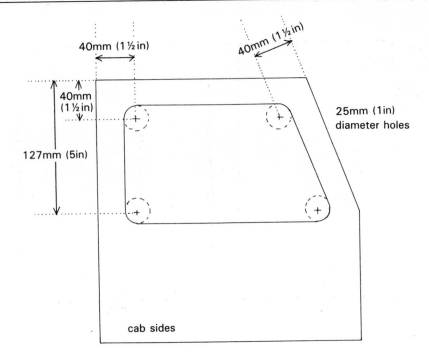

40mm (1½in)

40mm (1½in)

40mm
(1½in)

127mm (5in)

25mm (1in)
diameter holes

cab sides

Fig 5 Window position

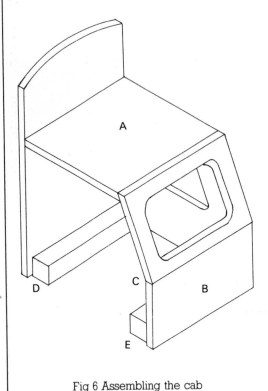

A

D

C

B

E

Fig 6 Assembling the cab

(clearance holes for no 6 woodscrews) into the back of the cab to correspond to the centre of the top of the truck back to enable the two units to be screwed together later.

Base
14 Make the base from a piece of 19mm (³/₄in) plywood (Fig 8). Round off the corners and sand the edges.
15 Drill eight 5mm (³/₁₆in) diameter holes (clearance for no 8 woodscrews) and countersink these on the underside. These holes must correspond to the positions of the bottom blocks in the cab and truck back.
16 Finally fit the castor plates to the underside of the base, keeping them near the corners.

Finishing
17 Screw the three sections of the truck together and then dismantle them before

colour photograph:
Truck (page 44) and Fire Engine (page 67)

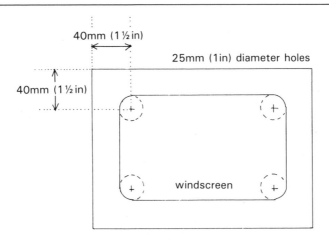

40mm (1½in)

40mm (1½in)

25mm (1in) diameter holes

windscreen

Fig 7 Cutting out the windscreen

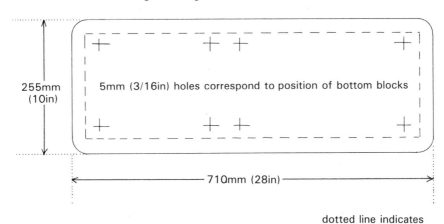

255mm (10in)

5mm (3/16in) holes correspond to position of bottom blocks

710mm (28in)

dotted line indicates cab and back position

19mm (¾in) plywood

castors

Fig 8 Baseboard and castor position

painting the separate pieces with non-toxic paint and varnish. Don't forget to fill any small pin holes and cracks before a final clean-up and sand prior to painting and varnishing. The cab may be decorated by painting on a bumper and radiator.

18 Reassemble the unit by using two 40mm (1½in) no 6 countersunk woodscrews and no

colour photograph:
Baby Walker (page 37) and Tricycle (page 60)

6 screwcups, to screw the cab to the back unit, and then use eight 40mm (1½in) no 8 countersunk woodscrews to screw the base to the assembled cab and back unit.
19 Fit the castors to the plates.

Note
This design may be slightly altered by adding a different back unit to make it into an open truck, still using the same cab and base.

Dog

This is a fun-to-make and a fun-to-use toy. Every child would like to have a pet and the design for this dog always proves to be popular. Don't be put off by the shape of the body; it is in fact very easy to make. Once covered in synthetic fur fabric or an off-cut of carpet the final effect is quite realistic. Castors are fitted for easy use.
(Shown in colour on page 87)

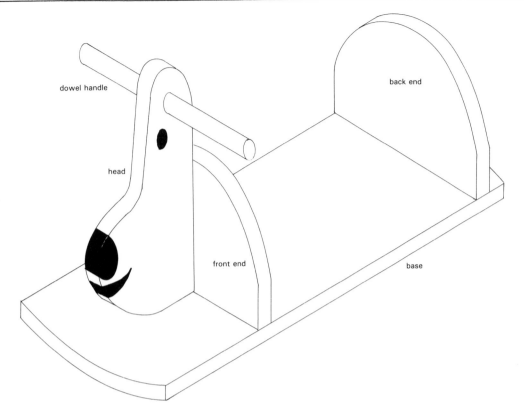

dowel handle

head

front end

back end

base

Fig 1 The assembled dog

Materials

Base	1	584 × 216 × 19mm(23 × 8½ × ¾in)	Planed softwood
Ends	2	216 × 178 × 19mm(8½ × 7 × ¾in)	Planed softwood
Head	1	333 × 152 × 19mm(13 × 6 × ¾in)	Planed softwood
Body	1	381 × 558 × 4mm(15 × 22 × 3/16in)	Birch plywood
Back support	1	305 × 227 × 12mm(12 × 9 × ½in)	Plywood
Handle	1	255 × 25mm diameter(10 × 1in)	Dowel

Piece of carpet or fur fabric to cover dog, approximately 381 × 558mm (15 × 22in)
4 × 45mm (1¾in) twin-wheeled plate-fitting castors
50mm(2in) no 8 countersunk woodscrews
32mm(1¼in) no 8 countersunk woodscrews
No 8 surface screwcups
19mm(¾in) no 6 roundheaded woodscrews (for castor plates)
25mm(1in) roundheaded wire nails
Carpet tacks
6mm(¼in) dowel
Wood glue
Non-toxic paint and varnish

1 Cut the base and two ends from the planed softwood, to the size and shape shown (Figs 2 and 3).

2 Drill nine 5mm ($^3/_{16}$in) holes, clearance for no 8 woodscrews.

3 Countersink these holes on one side of the timber. Clean up and glass-paper these pieces on the faces which are to be seen, prior to assembly.

4 Glue and screw the two ends to the base (Fig 2) using 50mm (2in) no 8 countersunk woodscrews, ensuring that they are square to the base, and that the end with the holes in (to take the head) is positioned to the front.

5 Cut out the shape of the head, using an electric jigsaw or coping saw, from some 19mm ($^3/_4$in) planed softwood (Fig 4).

6 Clean up the shape using a rasp or file and glass-paper.

7 Drill the 25mm (1in) diameter hole, to take the dowel handle, and then glue and screw the head to the front end using 50mm (2in) no 8 countersunk workscrews.

8 Form the body by bending a piece of 4mm ($^3/_{16}$in) plywood over the shaped ends. You will find that birch plywood is more pliable and less brittle than some of the mahogany-type plywoods, and there should be little difficulty in bending it over the ends. If birch plywood is not available, or if difficulty is experienced, it may be necessary to soak the plywood overnight in water.

Note

The grain of the plywood should 'run' in the short direction, ie from the head to the back of the dog.

9 Fasten the plywood in place using 25mm (1in) roundheaded wire nails. It is easier to start on one long edge of the base and gradually work round the curve. It will help at this stage if you can get someone to help hold the plywood down, round the curve, and then place the work in the vice, or hold it down with cramps, while you are nailing it down.

10 Allow the glue to set and then clean up any over-hanging edges and remove all sharp corners.

11 Cut and shape the back support from a piece of 12mm ($^1/_2$in) plywood and drill four 5mm ($^3/_{16}$in) holes (Fig 5). Glue and screw this in place at the back of the dog, using 32mm (1$^1/_4$in) no 8 countersunk woodscrews and no 8 screwcups.

12 Clean up a length of 25mm (1in) dowel and fit it into the hole already drilled in the head. Secure this in place by drilling a 6mm ($^1/_4$in) diameter hole through the head and into the dowel handle, into which a piece of 6mm ($^1/_4$in) dowel should be glued.

Finishing

13 Fit the castor plates in the corners of the underside of the dog and give it a final clean-up with glass-paper.

14 Apply three or four coats of varnish before painting on its nose, eyes and mouth with black gloss.

15 Cut a piece of fur fabric, or carpet, to fit over the body of the dog and staple or tack this in place. If you prefer you may use velcro tape to fasten the fur in place, to make it easier to remove for washing.

16 Finally fit the castors.

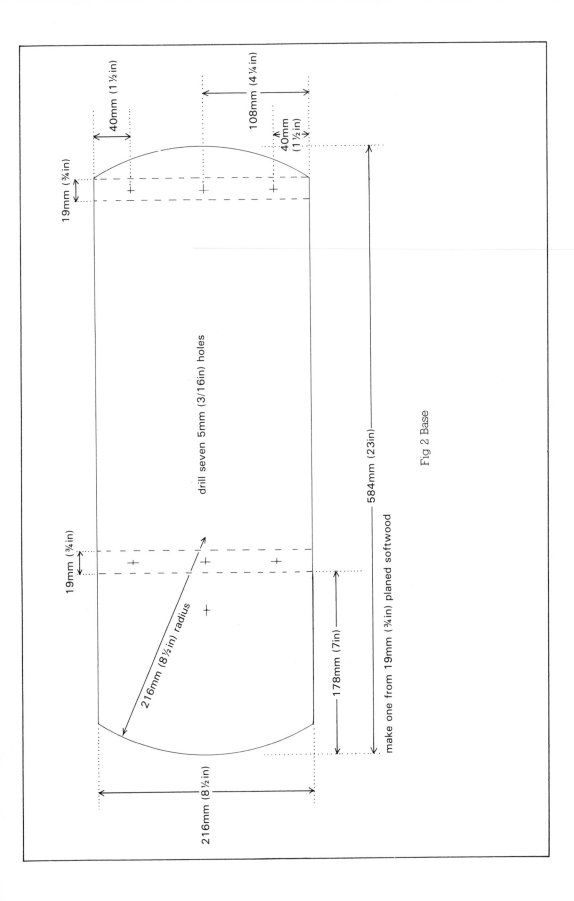

40mm (1½in)

108mm (4¼in)

40mm (1½in)

19mm (¾in)

19mm (¾in)

drill seven 5mm (3/16in) holes

216mm (8½in) radius

19mm (¾in)

178mm (7in)

216mm (8½in)

584mm (23in)

make one from 19mm (¾in) planed softwood

Fig 2 Base

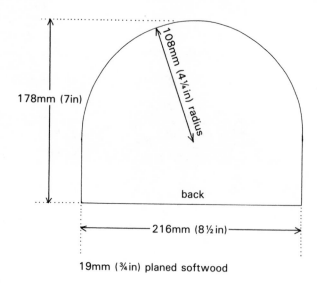

178mm (7in)

108mm (4¼in) radius

back

——216mm (8½in)——

19mm (¾in) planed softwood

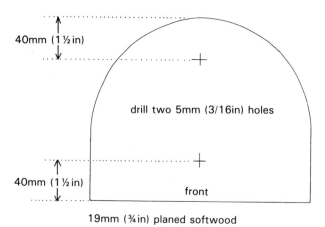

40mm (1½in)

drill two 5mm (3/16in) holes

40mm (1½in)

front

19mm (¾in) planed softwood

Fig 3 Cutting out the ends

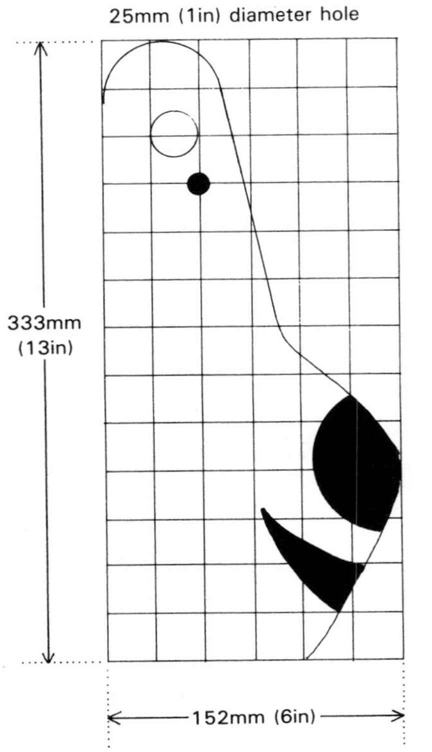

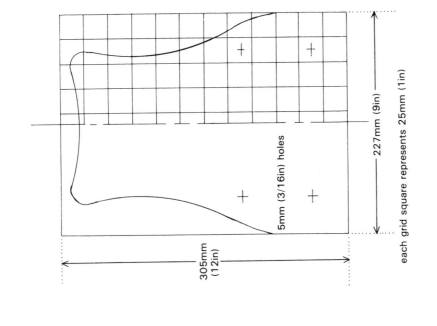

5mm (3/16in) holes

227mm (9in)

305mm
(12in)

each grid square represents 25mm (1in)

Fig 5 Cutting out the back support

25mm (1in) diameter hole

152mm (6in)

333mm
(13in)

each grid square represents 25mm (1in)
19mm (¾in) planed softwood

Fig 4 Head

Tricycle

This tricycle could well be the first form of transport for the younger child. The design is particularly versatile, you can enlarge the dimensions, in proportion, to make a larger version to suit children of up to eight years. Don't be put off by the detailed nature of this toy; it is easy to make in step-by-step stages. The steering column mechanism increases manoeuvrability and this tricycle will give your child hours of fun both inside the house and outdoors.
(Shown in colour on page 52)

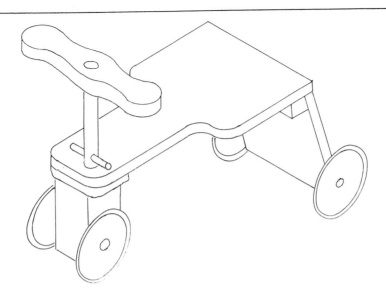

Fig 1 Assembled tricycle

Materials

Seat	1	380 × 216 × 19mm(15 × 8½ × ¾in)	Planed softwood
Back support	1	177 × 216 × 19mm(7 × 8½ × ¾in)	Planed softwood
Seat brace and axle block	1	460 × 45 × 45mm(18 × 1¾ × 1¾in)	Planed softwood
Steering block	1	150 × 75mm × 75mm(6 × 3in × 3in)	Planed hardwood
Handle	1	255 × 50 × 25mm(10 × 2× 1in)	Plywood
Steering column	1	250 × 25mm(11 × 1in)	Dowel
Seat front strengthener	1	100 × 100 × 19mm(4 × 4 × ¾in)	Plywood

4 × 100m (4in) diameter (or larger) plastic wheels
Axle approximately 460mm (18in) or steel bar to suit wheel bore
Steel washers
Sprung hub-caps
50mm (2in) no 8 countersunk woodscrews
32mm (1¼in) no 8 countersunk woodscrews
No 8 surface screwcups
6mm (¼in) dowel
Wood glue
Non-toxic paint and varnish

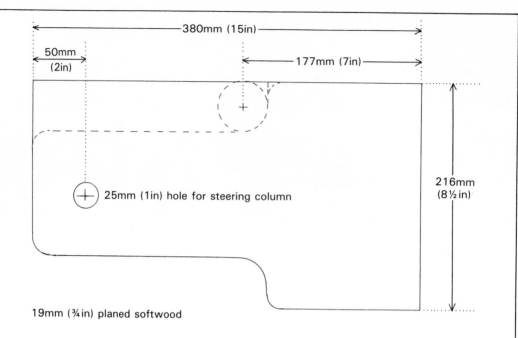

25mm (1in) hole for steering column

19mm (¾in) planed softwood

Fig 2 Seat

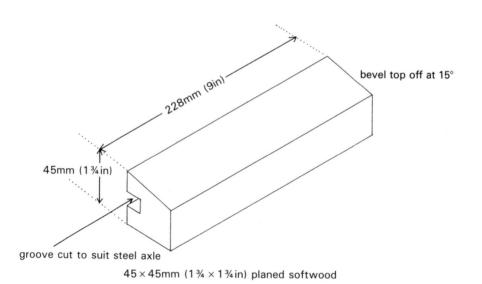

bevel top off at 15°

groove cut to suit steel axle

45 × 45mm (1¾ × 1¾in) planed softwood

Fig 3 Axle block

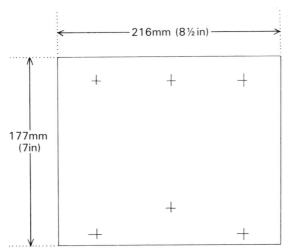

5mm (3/16in) diameter holes to suit
position of axle block and top brace

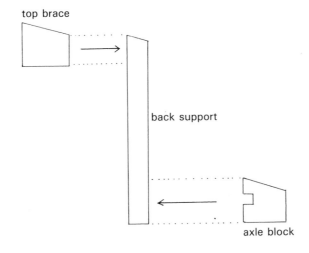

top brace

back support

axle block

Fig 4 Back support and blocks

1 Shape the seat from the 380 × 216 × 19mm (15 × 8$\frac{1}{2}$ × $\frac{3}{4}$in) planed softwood. If you have access to a 50mm (2in) hole cutter it is easier to drill two holes in the positions indicated (Fig 2) and then remove the remaining waste by sawing down the straight lines. If this method is not possible it will be necessary to cut the shape of the seat using an electric jigsaw or coping saw. Use a rasp or file and glass-paper to clean up the edges of the seat, removing all the sharp edges.

2 To strengthen the front of the seat, and to help prevent splitting, glue and screw a square of 19mm ($\frac{3}{4}$in) plywood to the front underside of the seat (Fig 5) using 32mm (1$\frac{1}{4}$in) no 8 countersunk woodscrews.

3 Drill a 25mm (1in) diameter hole through the seat (Fig 2) at the front to take the 25mm (1in) diameter dowel steering column at a later stage.

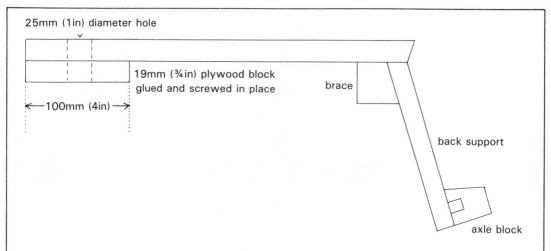

25mm (1in) diameter hole

19mm (¾in) plywood block
glued and screwed in place

brace

←—100mm (4in)—→

back support

axle block

Fig 5 Assembled seat and back support showing brace and axle block
screwed in place

4 Prepare the seat brace and axle block from about 460mm (18in) of 45 × 45mm ($1^3/_4$ × $1^3/_4$in) planed softwood, by planing it to an angle of 75°, and then cut off 200mm (8in) for the seat brace, and 230mm (9in) for the back axle block. This piece must be further prepared by ploughing a groove down its length to accept the axle (Fig 3). This may be done in several ways, either by using an electric router, a plough plane, or by taking several cuts out with a circular saw, providing you have access to one with a rise and fall table. If none of these methods are available, it is possible to make two saw cuts with a tenon saw, and then remove the waste using a wood chisel of the correct width.

5 Glue and screw the seat brace to the underside of the seat using 50mm (2in) no 8 countersunk woodscrews, ensuring that the angle is sloping outwards.

6 Prepare the back support from 178mm (7in) of 216 × 19mm ($8^1/_2$ × $3/_4$in) timber by planing one end to an angle of 75° to suit the slope on the seat brace.

7 Drill six 5mm ($3/_{16}$in) diameter holes (Fig 4), clearance for no 8 woodscrews. Clean up and glue and screw this piece in place using 50mm (2in) no 8 countersunk woodscrews and screwcups.

8 Carefully glue and screw the axle block to the back support, making sure that the groove is kept clear to accept the steel axle. Use 50mm (2in) no 8 woodscrews and screwcups (Fig 5). It may be advisable to drill pilot holes in the axle block to help prevent splitting when screwing in place.

9 Make the steering block from a piece of 75mm (3in) square by 150mm (6in) planed hardwood if available. Drill a 25mm (1in) diameter hole in the centre of one end to a depth of about 50mm (2in). Glue and peg about 250mm (10in) of 25mm (1in) diameter dowel into this hole (Fig 6). To get the position of the front axle hole it is better to put the back wheels on temporarily, and then assemble the steering block and seat. Hold the front wheel to the block and mark the position of the centre for the axle.

10 Shape the handle from a piece of 25mm (1in) thick plywood (Fig 7). If this is not available glue together two pieces of 12mm ($1/_2$in) plywood. Drill a 25mm (1in) diameter hole through the centre and shape the handle to form a comfortable grip. Use a rasp or file and glass-paper to remove all the sharp edges and corners.

Do not assemble the handle at this stage (see stage 13).

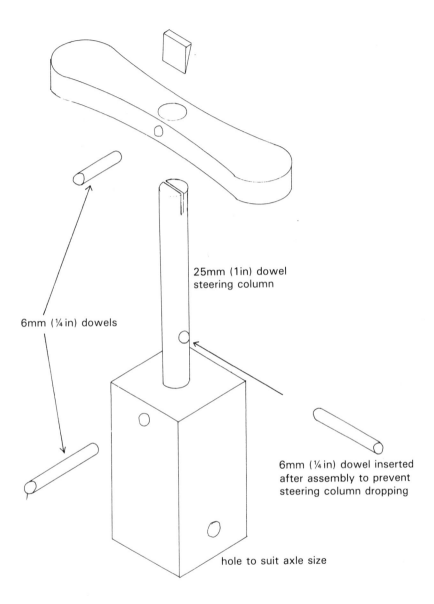

25mm (1in) dowel
steering column

6mm (¼in) dowels

6mm (¼in) dowel inserted
after assembly to prevent
steering column dropping

hole to suit axle size

Fig 6 Steering assembly

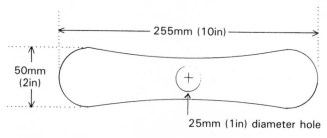

255mm (10in)

50mm
(2in)

25mm (1in) diameter hole

25mm (1in) plywood

Fig 7 Handle

Finishing

11 Clean up and varnish the seat unit and the steering column before attaching the wheels. Use sprung hub-caps to secure the wheels on the axles.

12 Cut a washer to fit on top of the steering block, out of an old polythene bottle to help reduce friction, and then fit the column through the hole in the seat.

13 Fit the handle to the top of the column (Fig 6). Make a saw cut in the top of the dowel to accept a wedge, and then drill a 6mm ($\frac{1}{4}$in) diameter hole through the handle and column, to take a 6mm ($\frac{1}{4}$in) dowel for extra security.

14 Drill a 6mm ($\frac{1}{4}$in) diameter hole through the 25mm (1in) dowel steering column, just above the seat, and peg it with about 50mm (2in) of 6mm ($\frac{1}{4}$in) dowel. This will prevent the column dropping down through the hole and trapping your child's fingers. (This dowel peg can be seen in Figs 1 and 6.)

15 Finally give the handle a clean-up and a coat of brightly-coloured paint.

Fire Engine

This is a robust toy ideally suited to 'fighting fires'. It is always popular allowing children (not just the boys) to live in their own little world and be part of an emergency team. It is particularly attractive combining both varnished and painted timber in one toy. The fire engine is constructed in sections and therefore straightforward to make and easy to assemble. It is fitted with castors making it both easy to ride on and suitable for use on most surfaces.

(Shown in colour on page 51)

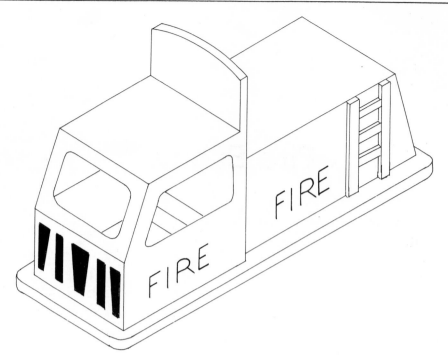

Fig 1 Assembled fire engine

Materials

Back Unit (Figs 2 and 4)

Sides	2	380 × 146 × 19mm (15 × 5³/₄ × ³/₄in)	Planed softwood
Top	1	333 × 197 × 19mm (13 × 7³/₄ × ³/₄in)	Planed softwood
Bottom blocks	2	159 × 45 ×45mm (6¹/₄ × 1³/₄ × 1³/₄) approx	Planed softwood
Back	1	200 × 180 × 6mm (8 × 7 × ¹/₄in) approx Plywood	

Cab (Fig 7)

Sides	2	255 × 255 × 12mm (10 × 10 × ¹/₂in)	Plywood
Back	1	380 × 216 × 12mm (15 × 8¹/₂ × ¹/₂in)	Plywood
Top	1	216 × 203 × 12mm (8¹/₂ × 8 × ¹/₂in)	Plywood
Front	1	216 × 127 × 12mm (8¹/₂ × 5 × ¹/₂in)	Plywood
Windscreen	1	216 × 152 × 12mm (8¹/₂ × 6 × ¹/₂in)	Plywood
Bottom blocks	2	190 × 45 × 45mm (7¹/₂ × 1³/₄in)	Planed softwood

Base (Fig 9)

Base	1	710 × 255 × 19mm (28 × 10 × ³/₄in)	Plywood

4 × 45mm (1³/₄in) twin-wheeled, plate-fitting castors
40mm (1¹/₂in) no 8 countersunk woodscrews
40mm (1¹/₂in) no 6 countersunk woodscrews

colour photograph:
Sack Cart (page 78) and Wheelbarrow (page 101)

19mm (³/₄in) no 6 roundheaded woodscrews (for castor plates)
No 6 surface screwcaps
50mm (2in) oval nails
40mm (1¹/₂in) oval nails
32mm (1¹/₄in) panel pins
25mm (1in) panel pins
12mm (¹/₂in) panel pins
Wood glue
Woodfiller
Non-toxic undercoat and gloss paints
Clear varnish
Thin strips of plywood to make the ladders

Back Unit

1 Cut the two sides from the 146 × 19mm (5³/₄ × ³/₄in) planed softwood (Fig 2). The angle of the slope to the rear of the fire engine is 75°.

2 Glue and nail the top to the sides using 50mm (2in) oval nails and then fit, glue and nail the two bottom blocks in place. These are made from 45 × 45mm (1³/₄ × 1³/₄in) planed softwood, one of which should be planed to an angle of 75° (Fig 3) to match the slope of the back.

3 Pin and glue a piece of 6mm (¹/₄in) plywood in place as the back using 25mm (1in) panel pins (Fig 4).

4 Punch in all the nails and pins and fill with a natural woodfiller and clean up and sand the whole unit before fitting the ladders.

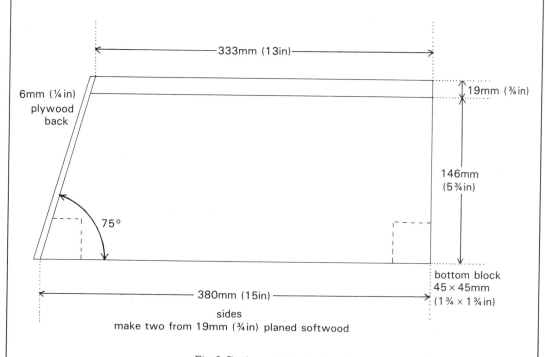

Fig 2 Cutting out the back unit

colour photograph:
Shopping Basket (page 94)

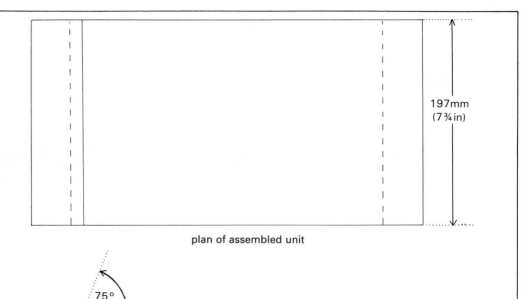

plan of assembled unit

197mm
(7¾in)

75°

Fig 2a Top showing angle

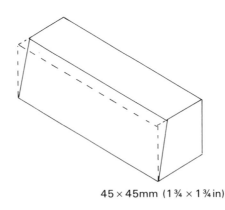

45 × 45mm (1¾ × 1¾in)

Fig 3 Detail of back block planed to 75° slope

5 Make the ladders from thin strips of ply-wood, their width is not critical, but should be in the region of about 6mm (¼in). These should be cut to the required length and sanded before pinning with 12mm (½in) pins and glueing in place on each side of the tank (Fig 4).

6 Make the cab from six pieces of 12mm (½in) plywood, and two pieces of 45 × 45mm (1¾ × 1¾in) planed softwood. Cut out the back, top, two sides, front and windscreen from the plywood (Fig 5).

7 Cut the windows in the side panels, by drilling four 25mm (1in) diameter holes, using a flat bit in an electric drill, in the positions indicated (Fig 6). Cut between the holes using an electric jigsaw or coping saw, but maintain the curve in the corners. Score the lines to be cut across the grain of the plywood with a marking knife, and saw just on the waste side of the lines. This will help to prevent the splitting of the face veneer of

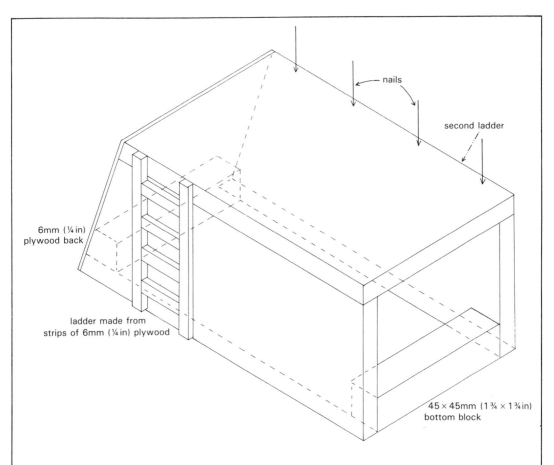

6mm (¼ in) plywood back

ladder made from strips of 6mm (¼ in) plywood

nails

second ladder

45 × 45mm (1¾ × 1¾ in) bottom block

Fig 4 Back unit

the plywood when cutting across the grain.

8 Clean up the sawn edges of the window apertures using glass-paper, and if necessary a rasp or file.

9 Glue and pin the cab together using 32mm (1¼in) panel pins which should be punched in and filled. Begin by pinning the back to the sides, followed by the top A and then the front B. The front edge of the top should be bevelled off to suit the slope of the front where the windscreen is to fit (Fig 7).

10 The size of the windscreen is determined by the length of the slope previously cut on the sides of the cab, and must be fitted accordingly, the bottom edge of which must be bevelled to fit the top edge of the lower front, indicated at C (Fig 7).

11 Cut the window out in a similar manner as described for cutting the windows in the side panels (Fig 8).

12 Glue and pin two pieces D and E of 45 × 45mm (1¾ × 1¾in) planed softwood to the inside of the cab (Fig 7). This is to enable the cab to be secured to the base at a later stage.

13 Drill two 4mm ($^5/_{32}$in) diameter holes (clearance holes for no 6 woodscrews) into the back of the cab to correspond to the centre of the top of the back unit to enable the two units to be screwed together later.

Base

14 Make the base from a piece of 19mm ($^3/_4$in) plywood (Fig 9). Round off the corners and sand the edges.

15 Drill eight 5mm ($^3/_{16}$in) diameter holes (clearance for no 8 woodscrews) and countersink these on the underside. These holes

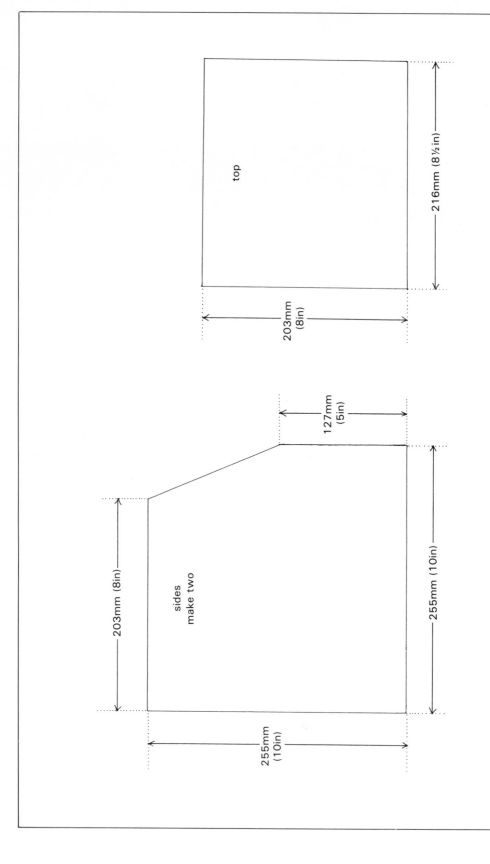

top

216mm (8½in)

203mm
(8in)

127mm
(5in)

sides
make two

203mm (8in)

255mm (10in)

255mm
(10in)

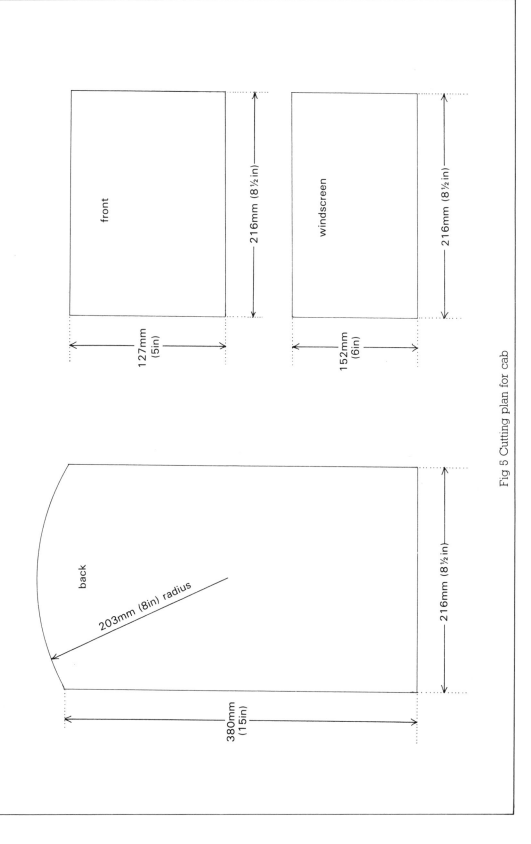

front

216mm (8½ in)

127mm (5in)

windscreen

216mm (8½ in)

152mm (6in)

back

203mm (8in) radius

216mm (8½ in)

380mm (15in)

Fig 5 Cutting plan for cab

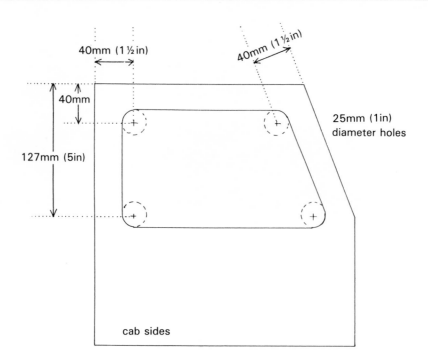

40mm (1½ in)   40mm (1½ in)

40mm

25mm (1in)
diameter holes

127mm (5in)

cab sides

Fig 6 Window position

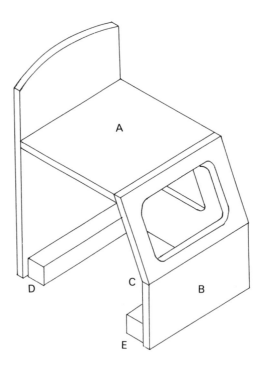

A

D   C   B

E

Fig 7 Assembling the cab

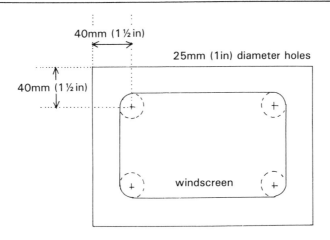

40mm (1½ in)

25mm (1in) diameter holes

40mm (1½ in)

windscreen

Fig 8 Cutting out the windscreen

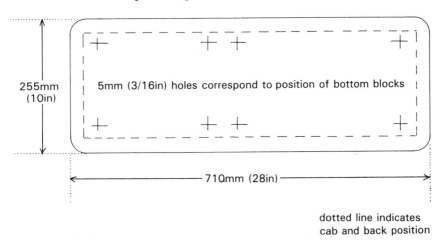

255mm (10in)

5mm (3/16in) holes correspond to position of bottom blocks

710mm (28in)

dotted line indicates cab and back position

19mm (¾in) plywood

castors

Fig 9 Base showing castor position

must correspond to the positions of the bottom blocks in the cab and back unit.

16 Fit the castor plates to the underside of the base, keeping them near the corners.

Finishing

17 Screw the three sections together, and then dismantle them before a final clean-up prior to painting and varnishing.

18 The word 'FIRE' should be painted on the cab side and on the back unit. Decorate the front of the cab by painting on the radiator and bumper.

19 Reassemble the unit by using two 40mm (1½in) no 6 countersunk woodscrews and no 6 screwcups, to screw the cab to the back unit, and then use eight 40mm (1½in) no 8 countersunk woodscrews to screw the base to the assembled cab and back unit.

20 Fit the castors to the plates.

Sack Cart

This toy is simplicity itself and very robust for both indoor and outdoor play. Children love to transport their toys around the house or garden and this sack cart always proves popular. You may even get some help around the garden! I chose to varnish my sack cart but you could, of course, paint it in bright colours.
(Shown in colour on page 69)

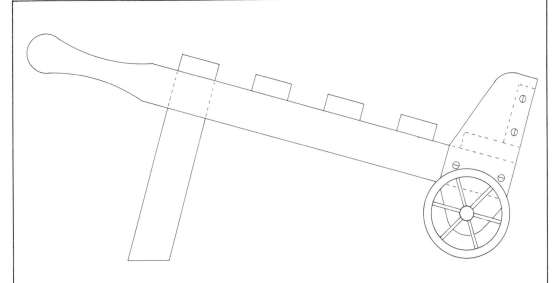

Fig 1 Assembled sack cart

Materials

Handles	2	610 × 45 × 19mm (24 × 1³/₄ × ³/₄in)	Planed softwood
Front rails	2	305 × 70 × 19mm (12 × 2³/₄ × ³/₄in)	Planed softwood
Rails	4	333 × 45 × 19mm (13 × 1³/₄ × ³/₄in)	Planed softwood
Legs	2	228 × 45 × 19mm (9 × 1³/₄ × ³/₄in)	Planed softwood
Axle supports	2	203 × 88 × 12mm (8 × 3¹/₂ × ¹/₂in)	Plywood

2 × 100mm (4in) plastic wheels
Approximately 380mm (15in) steel rod for axle to suit wheels
Sprung hub-caps
50mm (2in) no 8 countersunk woodscrews
40mm (1¹/₂in) no 8 countersunk woodscrews
32mm (1¹/₄in) no 8 countersunk woodscrews
No 8 surface screwcups
Wood glue
Clear varnish

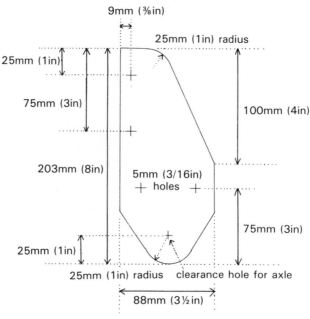

9mm (⅜in)

25mm (1in) radius

25mm (1in)

75mm (3in)

100mm (4in)

203mm (8in)

5mm (3/16in)
+ holes +

25mm (1in)

75mm (3in)

25mm (1in) radius   clearance hole for axle

88mm (3½in)

make two from 12mm (½in) plywood

Fig 2 Axle supports

1 Cut two axle supports from 12mm (½in) plywood (Fig 2).

2 Drill four holes 5mm (³/₁₆in) diameter, which is the clearance size for no 8 woodscrews.

3 Drill the axle hole in the position indicated (Fig 2), making the hole size to suit the size of axle to be used.

4 Sand the two pieces, removing all the sharp edges.

5 Shape two handles from two pieces of 45 × 19mm (1¾ × ¾in) planed softwood (Fig 3). Shape the hand grips using an electric jigsaw or coping saw, and smooth the shape down using a rasp or file, and glass-paper.

6 Cut out the two front rails from 70 × 19mm (2¾ × ¾in) planed softwood, and screw and glue them together using 50mm (2in) no 8 woodscrews (Fig 4).

7 Prepare the four rails from 45 × 19mm (1¾ × ¾in) planed softwood, 333mm (13in) long, by drilling a 5mm (³/₁₆in) diameter hole in each end of each piece (Fig 5). Using a smoothing plane, or glass-paper and block,

chamfer all the ends and corners (remove all the corners).

8 Sand down all the pieces prior to assembly.

9 To assemble the cart, glue and screw the axle supports to the handle using 32mm (1¼in) no 8 countersunk woodscrews and screwcups.

10 Screw the assembled front rails in place next, on top of the handles.

11 Space out and glue and screw the four rails in place, using 40mm (1½in) no 8 countersunk woodscrews and screwcups.

12 Prepare two pieces of 45 × 19mm (1¾ × ¾in) planed softwood (Fig 6) for the legs and glue and screw these in place using 32mm (1¼in) no 8 countersunk woodscrews and screwcups.

Finishing

13 Give the whole unit a thorough clean-up with glass-paper.

14 Apply three or four coats of varnish.

15 Fit the wheels using sprung hub-caps.

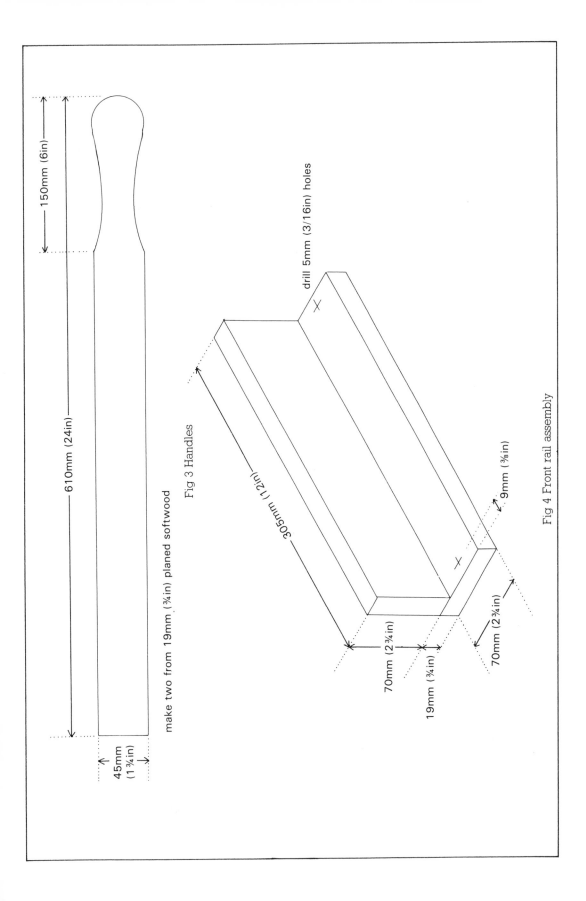

150mm (6in)

610mm (24in)

45mm (1¾in)

make two from 19mm (¾in) planed softwood

Fig 3 Handles

drill 5mm (3/16in) holes

305mm (12in)

70mm (2¾in)

19mm (¾in)

70mm (2¾in)

9mm (⅜in)

Fig 4 Front rail assembly

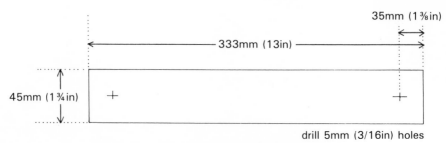

make four from 19mm (¾in) planed softwood

Fig 5 Rails

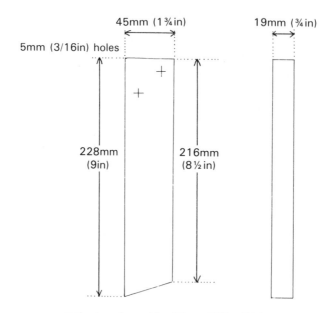

make two from 45 × 19mm (1¾ × ¾in) planed softwood

Fig 6 Legs

Tortoise

Very few children are lucky enough to own a tortoise due to import restrictions as they are now a protected species. Help your child's education and make this fascinating toy. The tortoise is strong and durable and easy to assemble. Paint it in realistic colours and it will be almost like the real thing!
(Shown in colour on page 87)

Materials

Base	1	$584 \times 216 \times 19$mm ($23 \times 8^{1}/_{2} \times {}^{3}/_{4}$in)	Planed softwood
Ends	2	$216 \times 178 \times 19$mm ($8^{1}/_{2} \times 7 \times {}^{3}/_{4}$in)	Planed softwood
Head	1	$356 \times 152 \times 19$mm ($14 \times 6 \times {}^{3}/_{4}$in)	Planed softwood
Body	1	$381 \times 558 \times 4$mm ($15 \times 22 \times {}^{3}/_{16}$in)	Birch plywood
Back support	1	$305 \times 227 \times 12$mm ($12 \times 9 \times {}^{1}/_{2}$in)	Plywood
Handle	1	255×25mm (10×1in) diameter	Dowel

4×45mm ($1^{3}/_{4}$in) twin-wheeled plate-fitting castors
50mm (2in) no 8 countersunk woodscrews
32mm ($1^{1}/_{4}$in) no 8 countersunk woodscrews
No 8 surface screwcups
19mm (${}^{3}/_{4}$in) no 6 roundheaded woodscrews (for castor plates)
32mm ($1^{1}/_{4}$in panel pins)
6mm (${}^{1}/_{4}$in) dowel
Wood glue
Non-toxic paint and varnish

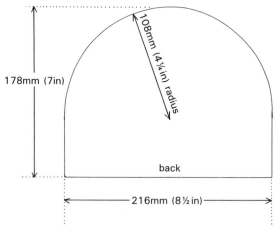

108mm ($4^{1}/_{4}$in) radius

178mm (7in)

back

216mm ($8^{1}/_{2}$in)

19mm (¾in) planed softwood

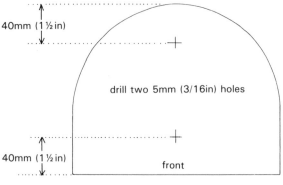

40mm (1½in)

drill two 5mm (3/16in) holes

40mm (1½in)

front

19mm (¾in) planed softwood

Fig 1 Cutting out the ends

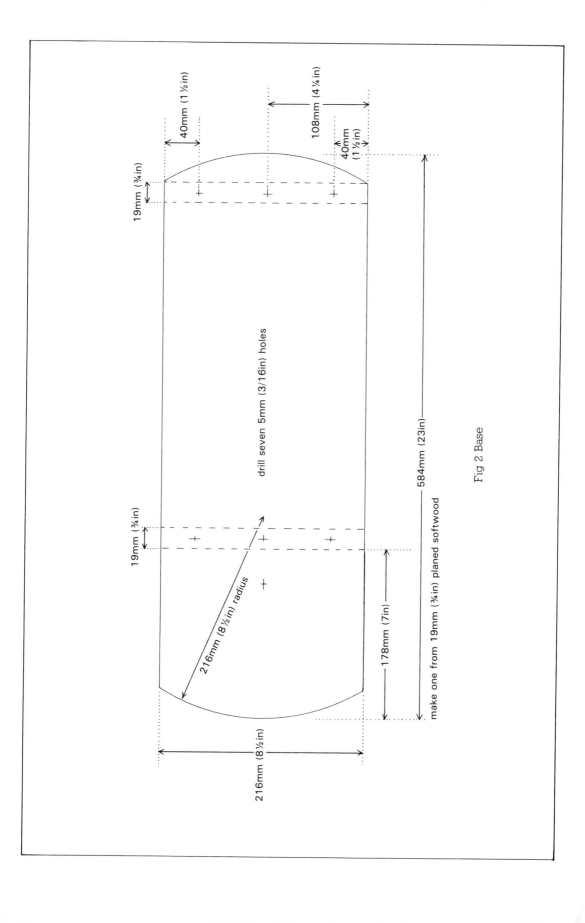

40mm (1½in)

108mm (4¼in)

40mm (1½in)

19mm (¾in)

drill seven 5mm (3/16in) holes

19mm (¾in)

216mm (8½in) radius

178mm (7in)

584mm (23in)

make one from 19mm (¾in) planed softwood

216mm (8½in)

Fig 2 Base

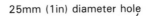

25mm (1in) diameter hole

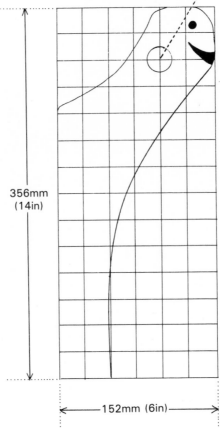

356mm
(14in)

←——152mm (6in)——→

each grid square represents 25mm (1in)

19mm (¾in) planed softwood

Fig 3 Cutting out the head

1 Cut out the base and two ends from the planed softwood (Figs 1 and 2).

2 Drill the 5mm (³/₁₆in) holes, clearance for no 8 woodscrews. Countersink these holes on one side of the timber. Clean up and glass-paper the faces which are seen.

3 Glue and screw the two ends to the base using 50mm (2in) no 8 countersunk woodscrews. Ensure that they are square to the base, and that the end with the holes in, to take the head, is positioned to the front.

4 Use an electric jigsaw, or coping saw to cut out the head from 19mm (³/₄in) planed softwood (Fig 3) and clean up the shape using a rasp or file and glass-paper.

5 Drill a 25mm (1in) diameter hole through the head to take the dowel handle, and then glue and screw the head to the front end using 50mm (2in) no 8 countersunk woodscrews.

6 Make the body by bending a piece of 4mm (³/₁₆in) plywood over the shaped ends. Birch plywood is more pliable and less brittle than some of the mahogany-type plywoods, and you should have little difficulty in bending it over the ends. If birch plywood is not available, or if difficulty is experienced, it may be necessary to soak the plywood overnight in water.

Note
The grain of the plywood should 'run' in the short direction, ie from the head to the back.

colour photograph:
Tortoise (page 83) and Dog (page 54)

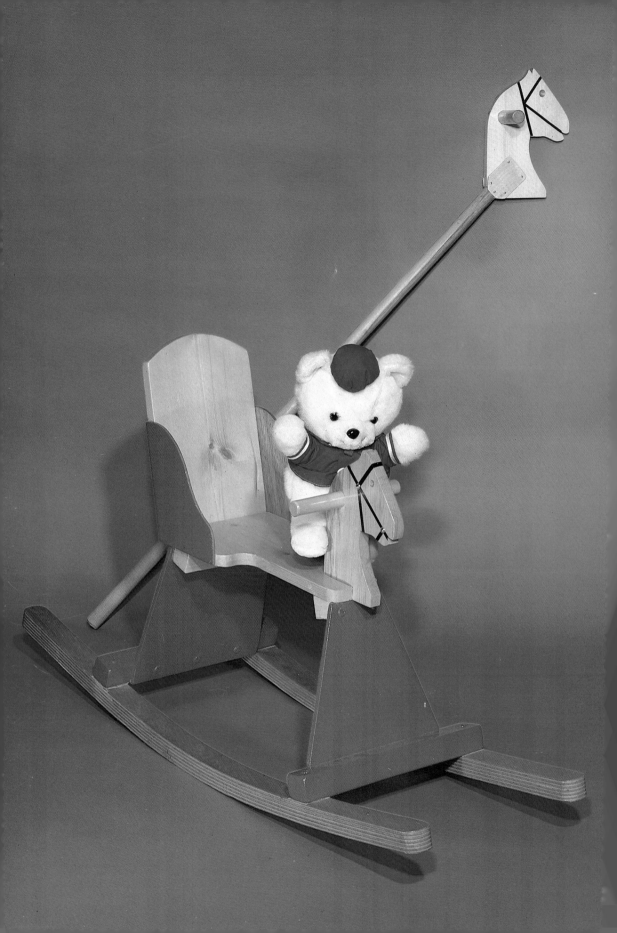

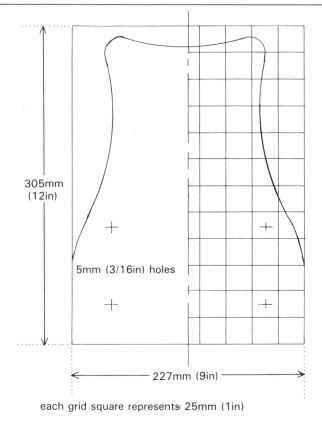

305mm
(12in)

5mm (3/16in) holes

227mm (9in)

each grid square represents 25mm (1in)

Fig 4 Cutting out the back support

7 Fasten the plywood in place by starting on one long edge of the base and gradually working round the curve. It will help at this stage if you can get someone to help hold the plywood down, round the curve, and then place the work in the vice, or hold it down with cramps, while it is nailed down with 32mm (1¼in) panel pins. Punch in the panel pins and fill the holes with a natural woodfiller.

8 After the glue has set clean up any over-hanging edges, remove all sharp corners and sand the body, since this is to be painted and varnished later.

9 From a piece of 12mm (½in) plywood cut and shape the back support and drill four 5mm (3/16in) holes as shown (Fig 4). Glue and screw the back support in place

colour photograph:
Hobby Horse (page 90) and Rocking Horse (page 108)

at the back of the tortoise, using 32mm (1¼in) no 8 countersunk woodscrews and no 8 screwcups.

10 Clean up a length of 25mm (1in) dowel and fit it into the hole drilled in the head. Secure this in place by drilling a 6mm (¼in) diameter hole through the head and into the dowel handle. Glue a piece of 6mm (¼in) dowel into this hole.

Finishing

11 Fit the castor plates in the corners on the underside of the tortoise using 19mm (¾in) no 6 roundheaded woodscrews.

12 Glass-paper the whole of the body.

13 Give the whole of the tortoise three or four coats of clear varnish and then paint the shell, with irregular-shaped scales using a dark-green, or brown paint. Paint the features on the head with black gloss, and then give the whole tortoise a final coat of varnish.

14 Fit the castors.

Hobby Horse

The hobby horse is always a popular toy. Children love to think they are the latest show jumping star! It is really simple to make once the head shape has been cut out.
(Shown in colour on page 88)

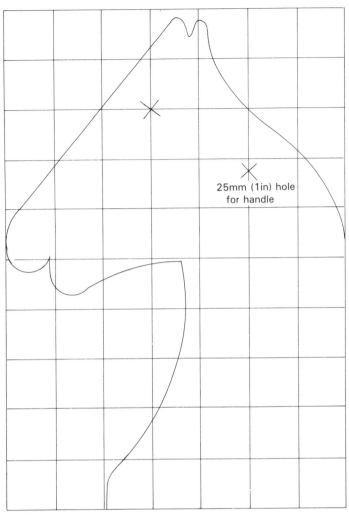

25mm (1in) hole
for handle

each grid square represents 25mm (1in)

Fig 1 Head

Materials

Head	1	255 × 178 × 19mm (10 × 7 × 3/4in)	Planed softwood
Broom handle	1		
Handle	1	255 × 25mm (10 × 1in)	Dowel
Plywood pads	2	50 × 75 × 6mm (2 × 3 × 1/4in) approx	Plywood

6mm (1/4in) diameter dowel
Panel pins
Wood glue
Clear varnish
Paint
Insulation tape

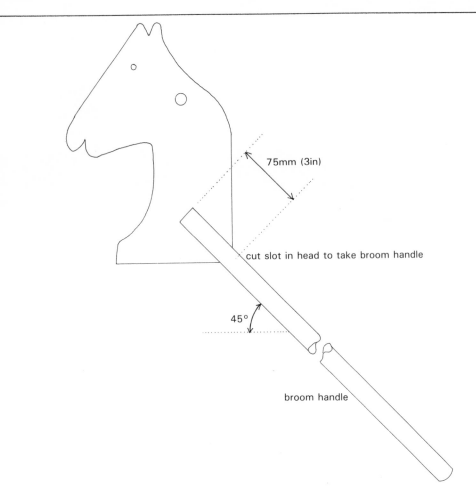

75mm (3in)

cut slot in head to take broom handle

45°

broom handle

Fig 2 Attaching the handle to the head

1 Cut out the shape of the horse's head (Fig 1) from a piece of 19mm (³/₄in) planed softwood and drill a 25mm (1in) diameter hole for the handle to be fitted later.

2 Cut a slot, at an angle of 45° to the square end (Fig 2). This slot should be the width of the thickness of the broom handle you are going to use and ought to be about 75mm (3in) deep. If the handle is thicker than the timber used for the head it will be necessary to plane two flats on it (Fig 3).

3 Secure the handle to the head by drilling a hole with a 6mm (¼in) diameter drill and place 6mm (¼in) dowel through the head into the broom handle (Fig 4).

4 Cut out and shape two 6mm (¼in) plywood pads. Glue and pin one on each side of the head over the broom handle for extra security (Fig 4).

5 Fit a piece of 25mm (1in) dowel through the head for the handle. The handle is held in place by drilling through both the head and the handle with a 6mm (¼in) drill. Peg this hole with a piece of 6mm (¼in) dowel and glue in place.

Finishing

6 Clean up thoroughly with glass-paper.

7 Apply three or four coats of varnish.

8 Decorate the head by using a countersink bit to make an impression for the eyes. The reins may be painted on or use thin strips of insulation tape and then varnish them over.

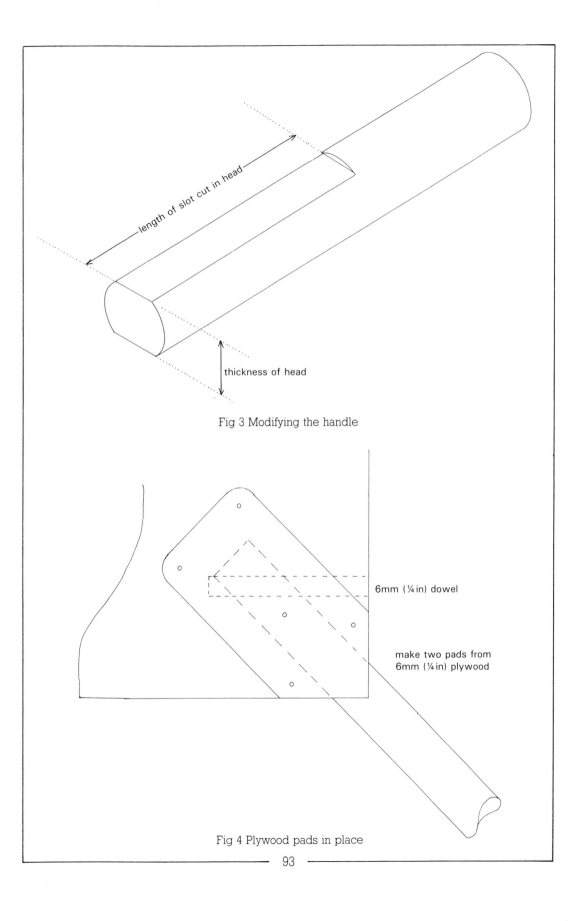

length of slot cut in head

thickness of head

Fig 3 Modifying the handle

6mm (¼ in) dowel

make two pads from
6mm (¼ in) plywood

Fig 4 Plywood pads in place

Shopping Basket

This toy has many uses, not only for carrying the shopping but for carrying other toys too. It is ideal for tidying the playroom and for storage – all the toys can be placed inside and then simply wheeled away. It is not difficult to make, just follow the step-by-step instructions.
(Shown in colour on page 70)

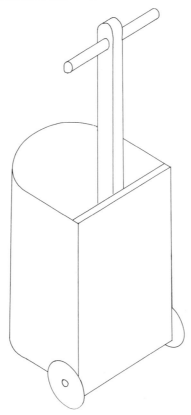

Fig 1 Assembled shopping basket

Materials

Base	1	255 × 255 × 19mm (10 × 10 × $^3/_4$in)	Plywood
Back	1	482 × 255 × 12mm (19 × 10 × $^1/_2$in)	Plywood
Body	1	686 × 381 × 4mm (27 × 15 × $^3/_{16}$in)	Plywood
Handle Support	1	762 × 45 × 19mm (30 × $1^3/_4$ × $^3/_4$in)	Planed softwood
Handle	1	255 × 25mm (10 × 1in)	Dowel
Axle Block	1	273 × 45 × 25mm ($10^3/_4$ × $1^3/_4$ × 1in)	Planed softwood
Foot	1	45 × 45 × 45mm ($1^3/_4$ × $1^3/_4$ × $1^3/_4$in)	Planed softwood

50mm (2in) no 8 countersunk woodscrews
45mm ($1^3/_4$in) no 8 countersunk woodscrews
40mm ($1^1/_2$in) no 8 countersunk woodscrews
32mm ($1^1/_4$in) no 8 countersunk woodscrews
No 8 surface screwcups
25mm (1in) panel pins
2 × 100mm (4in) diameter wheels, or larger
Approximately 333mm (13in) steel axle to suit wheels
Sprung hub-caps
6mm ($^1/_4$in) dowel
Wood glue
Woodfiller
Non-toxic paint

1 From the piece of 12mm (½in) plywood, cut the back of the basket to the size and shape shown (Fig 2).
2 Drill eight 5mm (³/₁₆in) diameter holes, which is clearance for no 8 woodscrews.
3 Sand each face and the top edge removing all sharp edges.
4 Cut the base from the 19mm (³/₄in) plywood.

5 Drill the 5mm (³/₁₆in) diameter holes shown (Fig 3).
6 Prepare the axle block from a piece of 45 × 25mm (1³/₄ × 1in) planed softwood by machining a groove down its length to accept the steel axle (Fig 4). This may be done in several ways, either by using an electric router, a plough plane, or by taking several cuts with

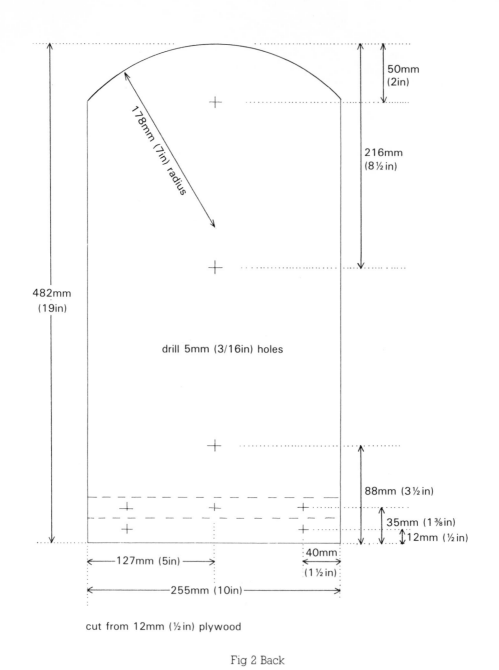

50mm (2in)

216mm (8½in)

178mm (7in) radius

482mm (19in)

drill 5mm (3/16in) holes

88mm (3½in)

35mm (1⅜in)

12mm (½in)

127mm (5in)

40mm (1½in)

255mm (10in)

cut from 12mm (½in) plywood

Fig 2 Back

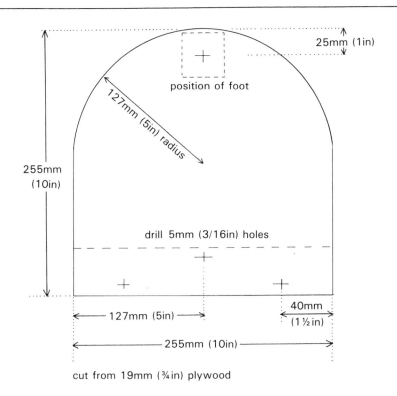

25mm (1in)

position of foot

127mm (5in) radius

255mm (10in)

drill 5mm (3/16in) holes

127mm (5in)

40mm (1½in)

255mm (10in)

cut from 19mm (¾in) plywood

Fig 3 Base

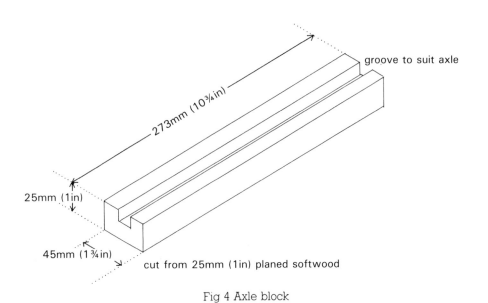

groove to suit axle

273mm (10¾in)

25mm (1in)

45mm (1¾in)

cut from 25mm (1in) planed softwood

Fig 4 Axle block

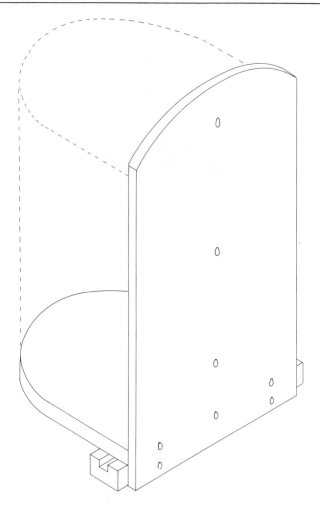

Fig 5 Assembled back and base showing axle block in place

a circular saw, providing you have access to one fitted with a rise and fall table. If none of these methods is available, it is possible to make two saw cuts with a tenon saw and then remove the waste using a wood chisel.

7 You will it find easier to glue and screw this block to the underside of the base before forming the body. Use 32mm (1¼in) no 8 countersunk woodscrews and screw cups taking particular care not to obstruct the groove (Fig 5).

8 Use 40mm (1½in) no 8 countersunk woodscrews and no 8 screwcups to glue and screw the back to the base and axle block (Fig 5).

9 Make the body of the basket from a piece of 4mm (³/₁₆in) plywood. The grain must run along the short dimension, ie from the top to the bottom of the basket. Before cutting the plywood to size it is advisable to measure the circumference of the body and allow about 6mm (¼in) extra for bending round the basket base.

10 Glue and pin the plywood body using 25mm (1in) panel pins, to the base and back. You will find it easier if you get someone to help with the bending and pinning of the plywood body.

11 Allow the glue to set and remove any overhang, clean the whole body up and punch in the panel pins, prior to filling with a suitable filler.

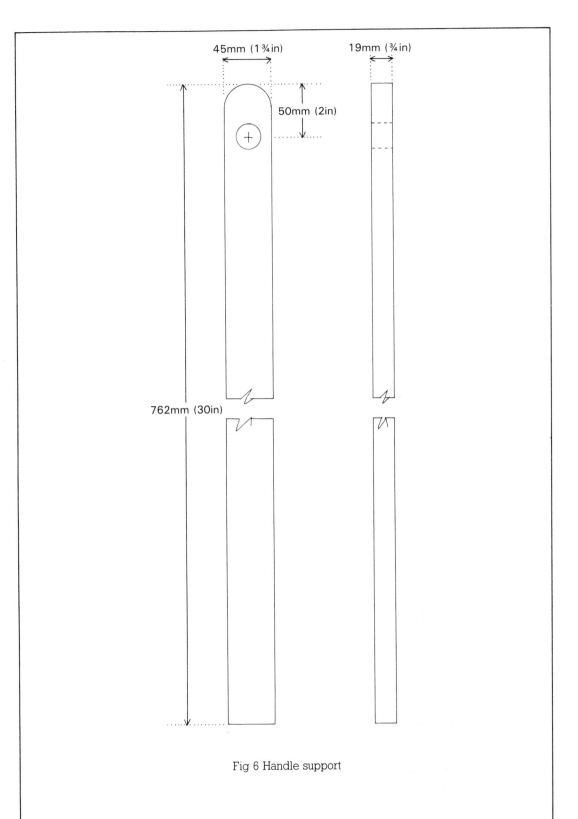

45mm (1¾in)

19mm (¾in)

50mm (2in)

762mm (30in)

Fig 6 Handle support

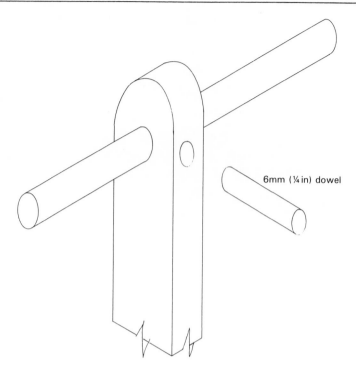

6mm (¼in) dowel

Fig 7 Securing the handle

12 Prepare a piece of 45 × 19mm (1³/₄ × ³/₄in) planed softwood for the handle support by rounding off the top and drilling a 25mm (1in) diameter hole for the dowel handle (Fig 6).
13 Insert 255mm (10in) of 25mm (1in) dowel into the hole in the handle support and secure this in place (Fig 7).
14 Clean up the handle assembly.
15 Glue and screw the handle assembly to the inside of the back, using 45mm (1³/₄in) no 8 countersunk woodscrews and screwcups.
16 Glue and screw the foot to the underside of the base to keep the basket upright when not in use. Position the 45 × 45 × 45mm (1³/₄ × 1³/₄ × 1³/₄in) block of planed softwood and screw in place using 50mm (2in) no 8 countersunk woodscrews. Adjust the size of this block if you are using larger wheels.

Finishing
17 Clean up the whole unit and remove all the sharp edges.
18 Paint with non-toxic paints.
19 Finally fit the axle and wheels, using sprung hub-caps to hold the wheels on the axles.

Wheelbarrow

This is not the easiest toy to make but once you have practised the techniques used in some of the other projects, there is no reason why you should not attempt to make the wheelbarrow. Fitting the front and back depends upon trial and error and a little patience! Just think how much pleasure this toy will bring your child when completed – it will be used endlessly indoors and out and be well worth the effort. Just varnish the wood or paint it in bright colours.
(Shown in colour on page 69)

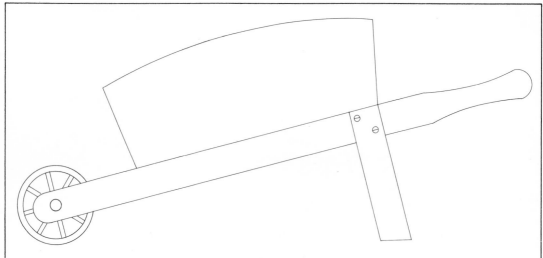

Fig 1 Assembled wheelbarrow

Materials

Base	1	343 × 280 × 6mm ($13^{1}/_{2}$ × 11 × $^{1}/_{4}$in)	Plywood
Sides	2	394 × 140 × 19mm ($15^{1}/_{2}$ × $5^{1}/_{2}$ × $^{3}/_{4}$in)	Planed softwood
Back	1	333 × 140 × 19mm (13 × $5^{1}/_{2}$ × $^{3}/_{4}$in)	Planed softwood
		approximate length only given, see text	
Front	1	255 × 140 × 19mm (10 × $5^{1}/_{2}$ × $^{3}/_{4}$in)	Planed softwood
		approximate length only given, see text	
Handles	2	711 × 45 × 19mm (28 × $1^{3}/_{4}$ × $^{3}/_{4}$in)	Planed softwood
Legs	2	191 × 45 × 19mm ($7^{1}/_{2}$ × $1^{3}/_{4}$ × $^{3}/_{4}$in)	Planed softwood

1 × 100mm (4in) or more diameter wheel
Approximately 150mm (6in) steel axle to suit wheel
Small off-cut of 25mm (1in) dowel
32mm ($1^{1}/_{4}$in) panel pins
50mm (2in) oval nails
32mm ($1^{1}/_{4}$in) no 8 countersunk woodscrews
No 8 surface screwcups
Natural woodfiller
Wood glue
Non-toxic clear varnish or paint
Sprung hub-caps

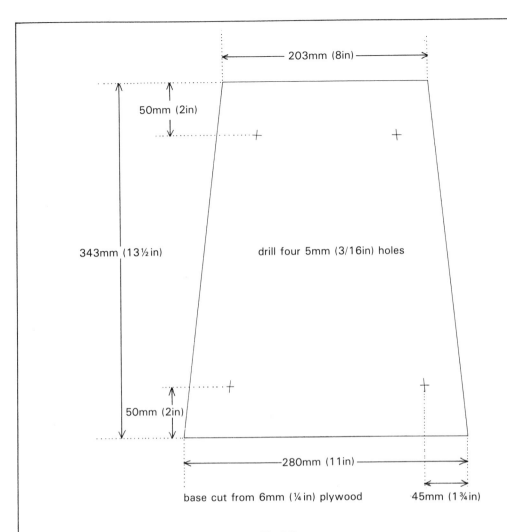

203mm (8in)

50mm (2in)

343mm (13½in)

drill four 5mm (3/16in) holes

50mm (2in)

280mm (11in)

base cut from 6mm (¼in) plywood

45mm (1¾in)

Fig 2 Base

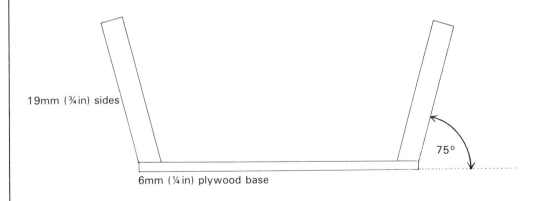

19mm (¾in) sides

75°

6mm (¼in) plywood base

Fig 3 Sides and base

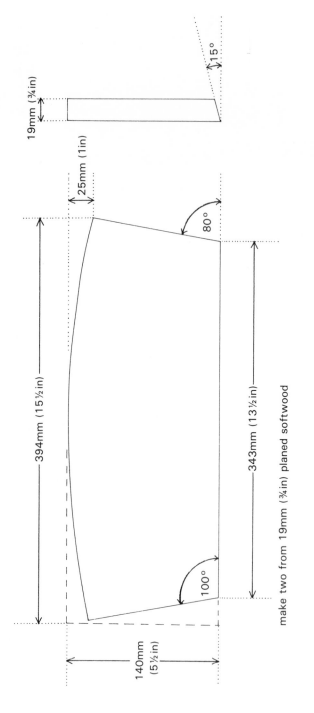

19mm (¾in)

15°

25mm (1in)

80°

394mm (15½in)

343mm (13½in)

100°

140mm (5½in)

make two from 19mm (¾in) planed softwood

Fig 4 Sides

1 Start by cutting the base from a piece of 6mm ($^1/_4$in) plywood, and drill the four 5mm ($^3/_{16}$in) diameter holes (Fig 2).

2 Using the two pieces of 140 × 19 × 394mm ($5^1/_2$ × $^3/_4$ × $15^1/_2$in) planed softwood for the sides, plane the bottom edge to an angle of 75° to allow the sides of the barrow to slope outwards (Fig 3).

3 Cut the two sides to the size and shape shown (Fig 4). The actual angle of the side is 100°.

4 Sand the inner faces thoroughly.

5 Pin and glue the sides to the base with 32mm ($1^1/_4$in) panel pins (Fig 3).

6 Plane the bottom edges of the 333 × 140 × 19mm (13 × $5^1/_2$ × $^3/_4$in) and 255 × 140 × 19mm (10 × $5^1/_2$ × $^3/_4$in) planed softwood, for the back and front, to an angle of 80°. No definite measurements for these two pieces can be given, the ones supplied are only a guide. The only satisfactory way to mark the size and shape of each piece, is by holding the timber in place and marking to size. Cut these pieces to length, just leaving the line on, and then plane them to fit each end of the barrow, so that a tidy fit is achieved. Shape the tops of each piece (Fig 5).

7 Clean up the inner faces thoroughly.

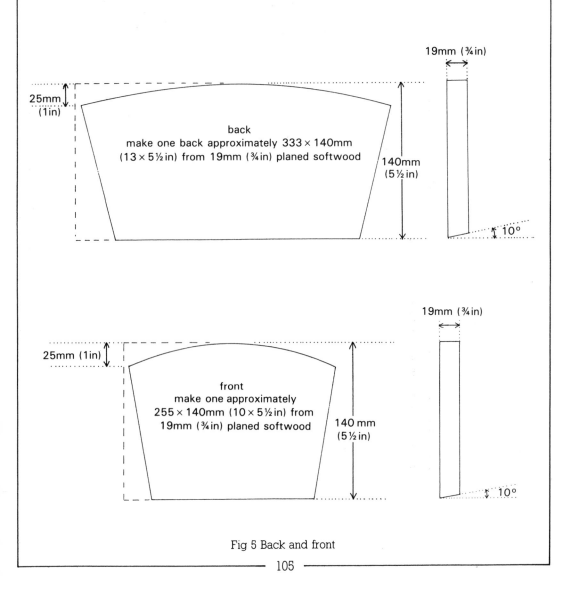

Fig 5 Back and front

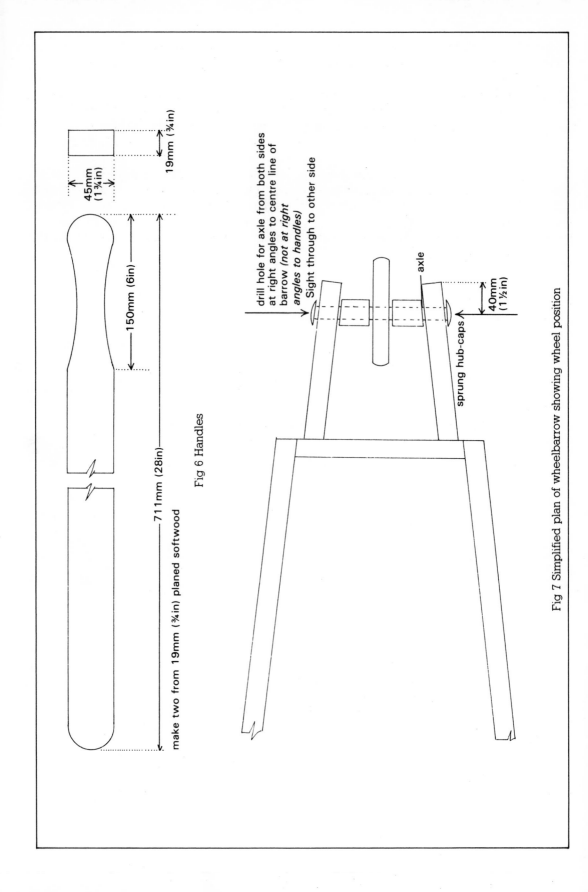

45mm
(1¾in)

19mm (¾in)

150mm (6in)

711mm (28in)

Fig 6 Handles

make two from 19mm (¾in) planed softwood

drill hole for axle from both sides
at right angles to centre line of
barrow *(not at right
angles to handles)*
Sight through to other side

axle

40mm
(1½in)

sprung hub-caps

Fig 7 Simplified plan of wheelbarrow showing wheel position

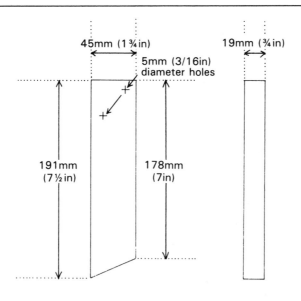

45mm (1¾in)

19mm (¾in)

5mm (3/16in)
diameter holes

191mm
(7½in)

178mm
(7in)

make two from 19mm (¾in) planed softwood

Fig 8 Legs

8 Glue and nail in place using 32mm (1¼in) panel pins to secure the front and back to the base and 50mm (2in) oval nails through the sides into the front and back. Punch in the nails and fill with a suitable natural woodfiller.

9 Use a smoothing plane to clean up the end-grains and then clean up the whole barrow body with glass-paper.

10 Shape the handles from the 45 × 19mm (1¾ × ¾in) planed softwood (Fig 6). Use a coping saw or electric jigsaw to cut the hand grips and then sand them to form a comfortable grip.

11 Clean up the handles with glass-paper.

12 Glue and screw the handles to the base using 32mm (1¼in) no 8 countersunk wood-screws and screwcups. Allow the handles to overhang the front of the barrow body by about 152mm (6in).

13 Mark out the position of the axle hole and drill from both sides (Fig 7).

14 Fix the wheel temporarily, making two spacers from the off-cuts of 25mm (1in) dowel.

15 Cut the two legs from some 45 × 19mm (1¾ × ¾in) planed softwood, shape the ends and drill two 5mm (3/16in) diameter holes (Fig 8). The length of these legs may be varied, and this will depend upon the size of wheel used and to some extent the age of the child who will use the toy.

16 Glue and screw the legs in place using 32mm (1¼in) no 8 countersunk woodscrews and screwcups.

Finishing

17 Remove the wheel and clean up the whole of the barrow, removing all sharp edges.

18 Apply three or four coats of varnish, or if preferred, paint the wheelbarrow in bright colours.

19 Finally fit the wheel using the sprung hub-caps to hold the wheels on the axles.

Rocking Horse

This is a lovely toy, one which will be treasured by any child. It suits children over a wide age range; the very young are supported by the design of the seat; the older child needs less assistance. It is one of the more difficult toys to make, but the techniques of, for example, laminating the rockers are well within the capabilities of the average DIY person. Follow the step-by-step instructions and you will get the satisfaction of not only making a unique rocking horse but watching the hours of fun your children will have playing with it.
(Shown in colour on page 88)

Materials

Jig (Fig 1)

Blocks	3	100 × 50 × 75mm (4 × 2 × 3in)	Planed softwood
Baseboard	1	1220 × 305 × 19mm (48 × 12 × $^3/_4$in)	Plywood
Seat	1	380 × 216 × 19mm (15 × 8$^1/_2$ × $^3/_4$in)	Planed softwood
Back rest	1	305 × 216 × 19mm (12 × 8$^1/_2$ × $^3/_4$in)	Planed softwood
Head	1	255 × 178 × 19mm (10 × 7 × $^3/_4$in)	Planed softwood
Side supports	2	228 × 203 × 6mm (9 × 8 × $^1/_4$in)	Plywood
Leg supports	2	280 × 280 × 12mm (11 × 11 × $^1/_2$in)	Plywood
Battens	from	1060 × 45 × 45mm (42 × 1$^3/_4$ × 1$^3/_4$in)	PSE
Handle	1	255 × 25mm (10 × 1in)	Dowel
Rockers	6	1140 × 115 × 6mm (45 × 4$^1/_2$ × $^1/_4$in)	Plywood

50mm (2in) no 8 countersunk woodscrews
45mm (1$^3/_4$in) no 8 countersunk woodscrews
75mm (3in) no 10 countersunk woodscrews
62mm (2$^1/_2$in) no 10 countersunk woodscrews
No 10 and no 8 surface screwcups
25mm (1in) panel pins
Wood glue
Non-toxic paint and varnish
Woodfiller

Jig

1 Start by making a jig to bend the plywood rockers. You need not use new wood if you are only making one horse as you will use the jig only once. Screw three blocks of wood, no more than 75mm (3in) wide, but at least 100mm (4in) deep to a baseboard in the positions shown (Fig 1).

Before using the jig, cover the areas which will come into contact with the rockers with masking tape or newspaper. Alternatively you may like to varnish and wax the jig to prevent the rockers from sticking to the jig.

Rockers

2 The rockers are made by laminating the six pieces of 6mm ($^1/_4$in) plywood, and cramping them onto the jig. Using a good quality wood glue, glue all the six pieces of plywood together and then cramp to the centre block of the jig (Fig 2).

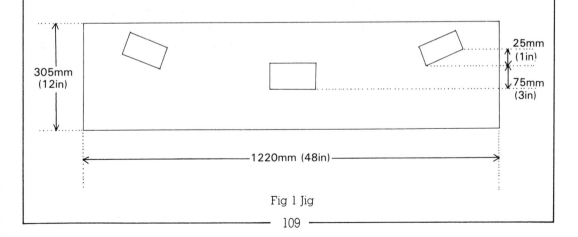

Fig 1 Jig

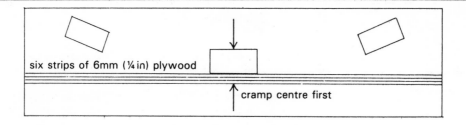

six strips of 6mm (¼in) plywood

cramp centre first

Fig 2 Positioning rockers on jig

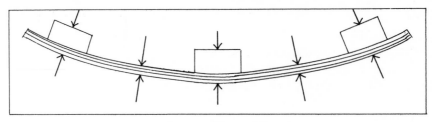

arrows show positions of G cramps

Fig 3 Cramping rockers on jig

3 Bend each end of the rockers round and cramp onto the end blocks of the jig. It may be necessary to add extra cramps between the three main cramping points (Fig 3).

4 Allow the rockers to set overnight and then remove from the jig.

5 Cut the 115mm (4½in) wide rocker in half and clean up to make two, 50mm (2in) wide. This is best done on a circular saw, or band saw. If these are not available I would suggest that you laminate two sets of rockers at just a little over 50mm (2in) wide and then clean up the edges. It may be necessary to plane the edges depending upon how evenly the rockers have been glued. It may be sufficient to sand them. In either case round off all the edges and corners and sand smooth.

Seat

6 Make from 380mm (15in) of 216 × 19mm (8½ × ¾in) planed softwood. Mark out the shape of the seat (Fig 4).

7 Use a 50mm (2in) hole cutter to cut two holes at position A and then cut out the shape of the seat. If a hole cutter is not available it will be necessary to cut the curves using a coping saw or an electric jigsaw.

8 Round off the two front corners and the two corners shown at B.

9 Cut the slot to take the head, 75mm (3in) deep and 19mm (¾in) wide.

10 Plane the back end of the seat at an

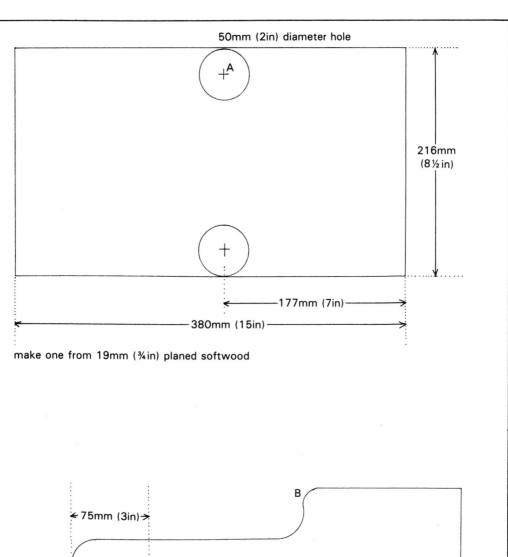

50mm (2in) diameter hole

+A

216mm
(8½in)

←—177mm (7in)—→

←————380mm (15in)————→

make one from 19mm (¾in) planed softwood

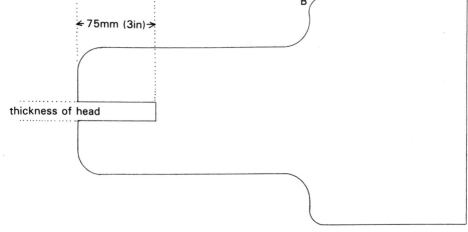

B

← 75mm (3in) →

thickness of head

Fig 4 Seat

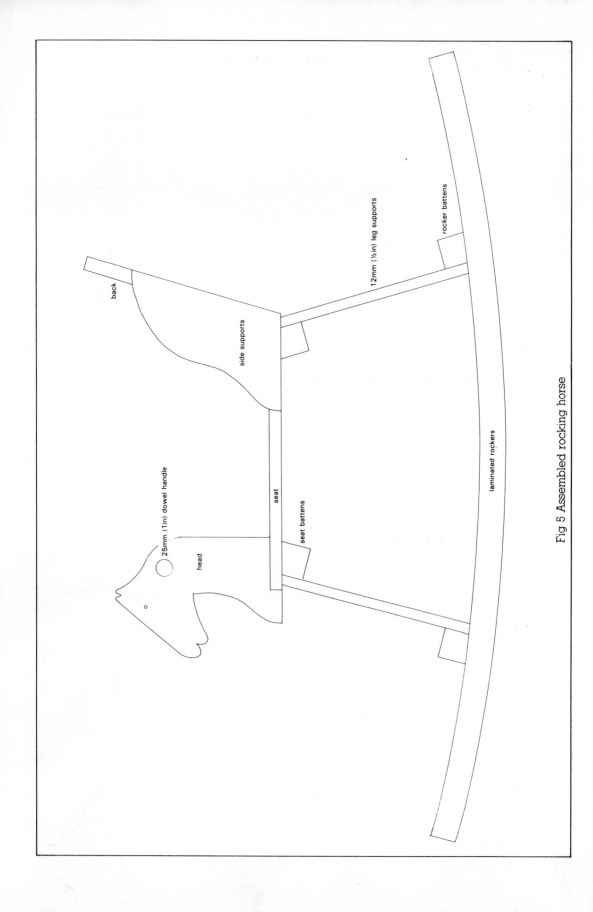

back

side supports

25mm (1in) dowel handle

head

seat

seat battens

12mm (½in) leg supports

rocker battens

laminated rockers

Fig 5 Assembled rocking horse

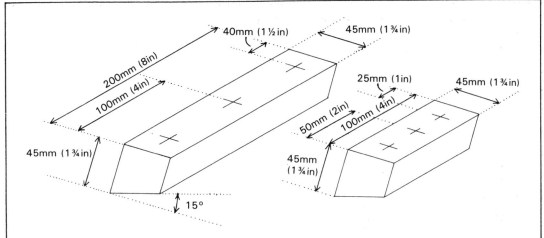

40mm (1½in)

45mm (1¾in)

200mm (8in)

100mm (4in)

25mm (1in)

45mm (1¾in)

45mm (1¾in)

50mm (2in)

100mm (4in)

45mm (1¾in)

15°

drill all holes 5mm (3/16in) diameter
except centre hole of smaller batten
which should be 5.5mm (7/32in),
countersink all holes

Fig 6 Seat battens

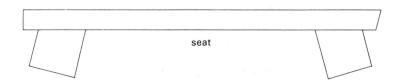

seat

Fig 7 Seat battens in place

angle of 75° so that the back rest slopes outwards (Fig 5).

11 Clean up all the edges and the shaping of the seat.

12 Prepare a batten from about 330mm (13in) of 45 × 45mm (1³/₄ × 1³/₄in) planed softwood. Plane or saw it to an angle of 75° and then cut one piece to the width of the seat at the back and one piece to the width of the seat at the front.

13 Clean up the ends and edges of these pieces and drill the holes shown (Fig 6).

14 Glue and screw the battens to the underside of the seat, using 50mm (2in) no 8 countersunk woodscrews (Fig 7).

15 Make the back rest from 305mm (12in)

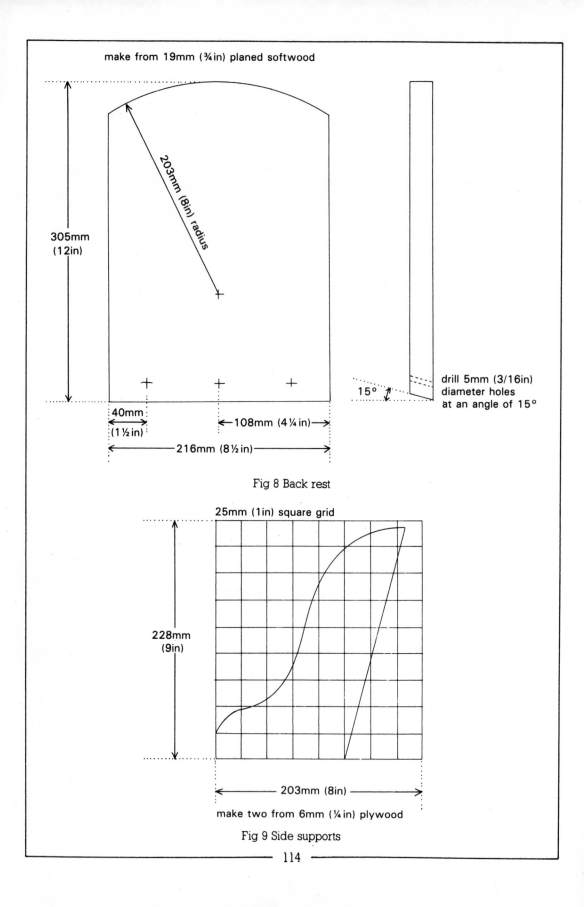

make from 19mm (¾in) planed softwood

305mm
(12in)

203mm (8in) radius

40mm
(1½in)

108mm (4¼in)

216mm (8½in)

15°

drill 5mm (3/16in)
diameter holes
at an angle of 15°

Fig 8 Back rest

25mm (1in) square grid

228mm
(9in)

203mm (8in)

make two from 6mm (¼in) plywood

Fig 9 Side supports

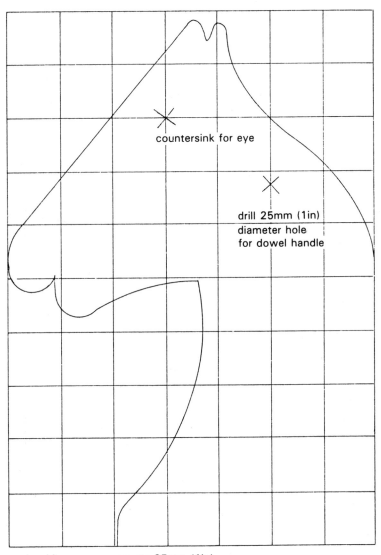

countersink for eye

drill 25mm (1in)
diameter hole
for dowel handle

each grid square represents 25mm (1in)
make from 19mm (¾in) planed softwood

Fig 10 Head

of 216 × 19mm (8$\frac{1}{2}$ × $\frac{3}{4}$in) planed softwood. Shape the top and drill the bottom (Fig 8).

16 Clean up the back rest and glue and screw in place using 50mm (2in) no 8 countersunk woodscrews and screwcups.

17 Cut the two side supports from 6mm ($\frac{1}{4}$in) plywood, clean up the rough edges and glue and pin them to brace the back rest to the seat with 25mm (1in) panel pins (Fig 9).

Head

18 Cut the head from 19mm ($\frac{3}{4}$in) planed softwood and drill a 25mm (1in) diameter hole to accept 250mm (10in) of dowel for the handle (Fig 10).

19 Drill through the head and dowel with a 6mm ($\frac{1}{4}$in) diameter drill and then glue in a 6mm ($\frac{1}{4}$in) diameter dowel peg to secure the handle.

20 Glue and screw the head in place using a 75mm (3in) no 10 countersunk woodscrew, through the centre hole in the front mounting block. Additional security may be achieved by drilling through the side of the seat into the head and pegging the hole with a 6mm ($\frac{1}{4}$in) dowel.

Leg supports

21 Cut two leg supports from 12mm ($\frac{1}{2}$in) plywood, planing the top edges to an angle of 75°.

22 Drill the 5mm ($\frac{3}{16}$in) diameter holes which is the clearance hole for no 8 wood-screws (Fig 11).

Assembly

23 Prepare the remaining 45 × 45mm (1$\frac{3}{4}$ × 1$\frac{3}{4}$in) planed softwood by cutting two pieces to 380mm (15in) long. Plane the bottom edge to an angle of 85°.

24 Drill a 5.5 ($\frac{7}{32}$in) diameter hole, clearance for no 10 woodscrews in the end of each piece, 25mm (1in) in from each end and in the centre of the width of the timber. These holes are to take the screws to fasten to the rockers at a later stage.

25 Glue and screw the leg supports to the battens, under the seat, using 45mm (1$\frac{3}{4}$in) no 8 countersunk woodscrews and screwcups.

26 Glue and screw the rocker battens to the lower ends of the leg supports with a 50mm (2in) overhang each side (this is the width of the rocker).

27 Use 62mm (2$\frac{1}{2}$in) no 10 countersunk woodscrews and screwcups to glue and screw the assembled horse centrally to the rockers.

Finishing

28 Clean up the whole of the horse with glass-paper making sure that all the sharp edges are removed.

29 Paint your own design onto the horse and apply three or four coats of varnish.

30 Decorate the head by using a counter-sink drill to make impressions for the eyes; the reins may be painted on, or thin strips of insulation tape may be used and then varnished over.

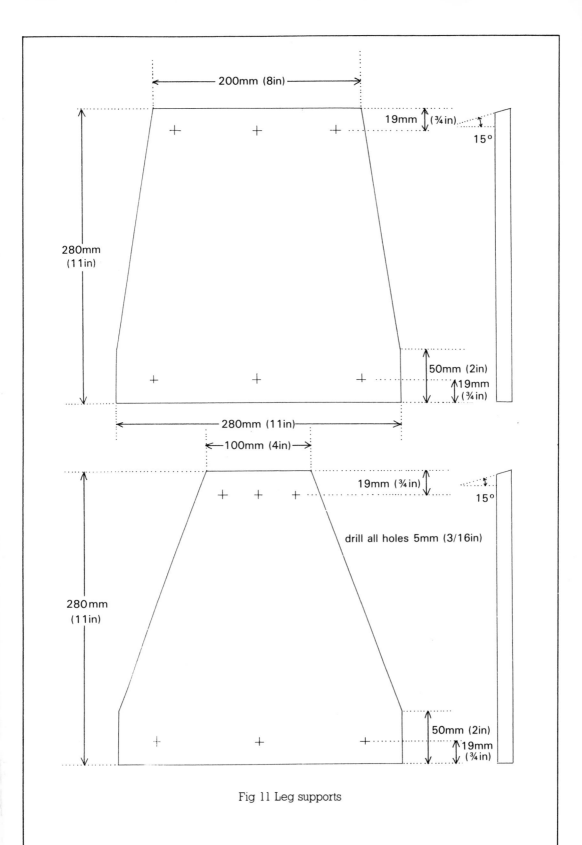

200mm (8in)

19mm (¾in)

15°

280mm
(11in)

50mm (2in)

19mm
(¾in)

280mm (11in)

100mm (4in)

19mm (¾in)

15°

drill all holes 5mm (3/16in)

280mm
(11in)

50mm (2in)

19mm
(¾in)

Fig 11 Leg supports

Index

Router, 32, 40, 64, 96

Sack cart, 69, 78
Sash cramp, 10
Screw cups, 15
Screws, 15
Shopping basket, 71, 94
Sliding bevel, 12
Smoothing plane, 9
Steering assembly, 65
Stickers, 7
Surform, 10

Tenon saw, 9, 21, 32
Tortoise, 83, 87
Train, 17, 33

Transfers, 7
Transformer, 14
Tricycle, 52, 60
Truck, 44, 51
Try square, 12

Varnishing, 15
Vice, 10

Warrington hammer, 12
Wedge, 20, 65
Wheelbarrow, 69, 101
Wheels, 15, 36, 42, 66, 80, 100, 107
Windows, cutting of, 47, 50, 72, 73, 76, 77
Wood chisel, 9
Wood filler, 15